LIVING WITH THE WHIDDY DISASTER

LIVING WITH THE
WHIDDY DISASTER

Brian McGee

DROMBEG BOOKS

ISBN: 978-0-9931143-2-8

DROMBEG BOOKS
Ballyhillow, Leap, County Cork, Ireland
Tel: 353 1 87 2720028
email: drombegbooks@gmail.com

The photographs of the Betelgeuse and the jetty

were taken by the late Ian Vickery

To Eleanor, Jacinta, Sonya,
Damien and Helena.

Foreword

THE PURPOSE OF this book is to give voice to one man's experience of Ireland's worst maritime disaster, when fifty people died in the early hours of 8 January 1979 after a fire broke out aboard the *Betelgeuse*, a French-owned oil tanker, at the Gulf Oil Terminal in Bantry Bay. The fire, by all accounts, was at first a small one but then spread rapidly to erupt into a massive fireball accompanied by an explosion that cast debris far and wide and reverberated as far as fifty miles away throughout West Cork.

Brian McGee was one of five Gulf workers who fought relentlessly and at great personal risk for many hours to stop the fire spreading to the twelve large oil tanks at the terminal, where a further explosion would have had catastrophic results for the town of Bantry. In the thirty-five years since he has often been reminded that he should be grateful for having survived, unlike seven of his co-workers; this is something he accepts, but he has also learned that there is more than one way to be robbed of one's life.

Brian and his co-workers gave little thought to their own personal safety that night as they fought non-stop for more than eight hours to prevent the fire from spreading. In the immediate aftermath, however, the horror of that night began to take its toll, and Brian quickly descended, as if falling over an unseen precipice, into a mental hell that he would have to endure for many years and which brought him close on a number of occasions to suicide. There has been recovery, as anyone who knows him recognises. This eventually came through a new-found spirituality and a rediscovery of faith, but only after a tortuous struggle that took him up a series of blind alleyways in search of a solution. And yet the scars are still there, and the experience of that night still lives within him; seared deeply into his mind is the image of men he knew well running for their lives along the terminal jetty as the flames engulfed them.

"I cannot be what I was," he says of his current situation, "but I can hold on to what is left and hope that it sees me through the rest of my life. Sometimes, however, it is like trying to hold on to smoke."

It is now clear with the benefit of hindsight that Brian suffered severely from a classic case of post-traumatic stress disorder (PTSD). A great part of his story is in fact concerned with the failure of the professionals to diagnose this and to treat him accordingly. And what now seems even more amazing is the fact that no one in authority, whether Gulf management, trade union representative or government official, had the vision or the sympathy to realise that those who had out their lives at risk over a protracted period might be in need of psychological support immediately afterwards. Self-protection, however, seemed to be the dominating concern after the disaster, so that those who could have helped chose not, or at least were blind to this particular moral duty.

The official account of what happened that night,

and one that future historians will first turn to, is contained in the mammoth 488-page report issued by the tribunal of inquiry that the government established just weeks after the disaster. The tribunal was led by Declan Costello, a High Court judge who had been a Fine Gael TD for twenty years and Attorney General for two years. His reputation as a jurist and as a forward-looking politician who was responsible for *Towards A Just Society*, a document that had a great impact on Irish political thinking in the 1960s, ensured that both the conduct of the tribunal and its findings were largely beyond criticism. And yet, not everyone close to the tribunal was happy, as evidenced by the resignation of Dr HK Black as scientific assessor to the tribunal because of the methods of investigation being employed; it is significant that this resignation, though reported widely, failed to prompt a compliant media to raise some pertinent and obvious questions about the conduct of the tribunal hearings.

Dr Black's main problem, which is examined at length later in this book, was essentially that the hearings were combative, forming a battleground for lawyers representing parties whose overriding objective was to deny, or at least minimise, their role in contributing to the disaster and thus avoid, or again minimise, the financial liabilities arising from damages. Can the whole truth really emerge from such a process? It is worth noting Brian McGee's own experience as a tribunal witness. He initially had a lot of hope – naively, he now admits – that the inquiry would provide some sort of closure for him and others and thus be part of a necessary healing process. His experience on the witness stand, however, was a deeply frustrating one; as someone with just a basic formal education and at that point quite mentally low, he felt intimidated by the whole proceedings and was unable to articulate what he believed was valuable information about what had happened on Whiddy Island that night. To arrive at the truth about something surely requires that everything be taken into account and everyone listened to with due attention, with allowances being made for those at a disadvantage, but such an approach was not, of course, possible in an adversarial process where high stakes were involved.

A Swahili proverb says that "When elephants fight,

it is the grass that gets trampled." For Brian McGee, what got trodden underfoot at the tribunal was not just his own sense of dignity as a person but much of the truth and with it the reputation of one man, John Connolly, who was in charge of the terminal control room on the night of the disaster. Connolly, who was subjected to intense cross-examination while on the stand and at one point broke down, was singled out by the tribunal findings as the person who had to shoulder much of the blame for the failure to save the lives of some, if not all, of those who had died.

For Brian McGee, this is not just incorrect, but it also served at the time to deflect the focus from where it should have been: the clear culpability of Gulf Oil for the low safety standards in operation for a long time at the terminal. The findings drew a detailed picture of Connolly's actions on the night that was accepted unquestioningly by the media, but it is worth noting that this picture was not based on direct evidence (the direct evidence to the contrary being dismissed out of hand) but was inferred. If Connolly, as Brian McGee believes, was unjustly treated by the tribunal, it must also be said that he was a victim of manipulation by Gulf Oil management, who put him into an impossible position about the time of the fire to suit their own ends. Brian himself, as he explains in this book, had a lot of pressure put on him in a threatening fashion to remain quiet about certain aspects of operations at the terminal, and he has sympathy for the situation John Connolly found himself in with the management.

As well as finding against Total, the French oil conglomerate that owned the *Betelgeuse*, and Gulf Oil, the tribunal strongly criticised the government for its failure to introduce regulations, as it had promised to do, governing safety and emergency operations at the terminal. This aspect of the findings never got the attention it deserved at the time, and it was certainly something that a more alert media would have followed up at some stage, given that it was a clear example of gross political and administrative negligence and a contributory factor to the extent of the tragedy. In many ways it was part of a theme that ran through the whole story of Gulf's involvement in Bantry from the beginning: an attitude of total indifference that allowed a multinational company to use the resources of Bantry Bay without being required to pay harbour fees and also left that company to its own devices regarding environmental protection (which a number of oil spills showed to be inadequate) and management of safety and emergency procedures to protect the lives of its workers and others using the terminal. The arrival of Gulf in Bantry Bay in the mid-1960s provided an unprecedented cash injection, particularly during construction, into a hard-hit local economy, and there was a lot of optimism at the time that it was just the beginning of greater things, with the possibility of a full-scale refinery even being raised. The reluctance to look too closely at this glittering prize or to question it was therefore somewhat understandable, but it was still unacceptable. There would be too high a price to pay.

Maurice Sweeney
October 2014

Contents

Beginnings

LIFE WAS GOOD, and life was full of possibilities. I was thirty-two years of age and had been working on Whiddy Island for ten years, first with a company called Rockfall, which was involved in marine drilling and blasting, and then as a general operator with Gulf Oil when the terminal was up and running.

The first job on Whiddy had come like a bolt out of the blue. I was working on the family farm in Donegal when a telegram arrived from my brother Charlie who was working for Rockfall, telling me to ring him urgently. After cycling the two miles to the nearest phone, I rang him, and he told me there was a job there for me if I wanted it. My parents were unhappy about me leaving, and my father said he would leave me the farm if I stayed. I didn't, and the next day I arrived in Bantry.

I had tried my hand at a few things before that. After leaving school at 14 I got a job in a bakery but gave up on it because, although I didn't mind baking bread, I hated having to mix dough. My mother, who didn't like losing a wage packet coming into the house, then marched me straight up to a drapery shop where she had arranged another job. I had to do billings and invoices, which was difficult as I had never learned to read and write properly at school because, although I was left-handed, I was forced to write with my right hand, which went completely against the grain. I winged it as best I could at the shop, however, and managed to remain there for four years. After that I headed to England where I worked in Middlesbrough for two years before returning home to work with a local builder and to help my father out on the farm. I had been a year at home when Charlie's telegram arrived.

It was never my intention to settle in Bantry. My

plan from the day I arrived was to work hard, restrict my social life, and return to Donegal with a decent amount of savings. But two things put a hold on all of that. The first was the offer of a job with Gulf Oil which followed soon after I finished with Rockfall and which was hard to turn down, but even more importantly there was Eleanor. We hit it off immediately when we first met and we were married in September 1968.

After a while I managed with a bit of luck to put two loans together that enabled us to buy a house, and it was this, along with the arrival of our first child, that made us decide to put our roots down in Bantry.

After working at the terminal for eight years, where most of my time was spent on the jetty, I was able to negotiate a shift change and was also soon afterwards promoted to assistant pump operator. It was rewarding to know that the company thought of me as a good employee.

As the New Year arrived in 1979, things were beginning to look even better. Eleanor and I now had three children and I had managed to make some dent in the two loans for the house. I had always been interested in construction and I was beginning to put together a plan to launch out on my own in the building trade. I felt the time would soon arrive when I could spread my wings. Life indeed was full of possibilities.

A night of terror

AT EIGHT O'CLOCK on the Sunday evening of 7 January 7 1979, I arrived at the terminal for my normal twelve-hour shift. Five of us were working on the island that night: myself as assistant pump operator, Johnny Downey as pump operator, Jim Kearns and Patrick O'Donnell, who were security men, and John Connolly, who was the controller overseeing all operations at the terminal and to whom everyone reported.

Five others travelled out with us on the ferry to take up duty on the jetty: Tim Kingston, who was the pollution control officer, Denis O'Leary, the security man, Jim O'Sullivan, a full-time utility man who was stand-in jetty foreman that night, and Charles Brennan, Liam Shanahan and Cornelius O'Shea, who were part of the jetty crew and worked part-time on relief shifts.

Jim O'Sullivan had got married only five weeks previously. Charles Brennan was working that night after swapping with someone else so that he could attend a dinner dance with his girlfriend the following Friday night.

Liam Shanahan was unaware as he landed at the jetty that his wife had gone into labour and would give birth to a baby boy that night. According to one story, Liam had explained to management about his wife's situation but was told he could forget about getting any more shifts if he did not come in that night. Some time before this, he had a dispute with the company about overtime payments, which he won, but this had resulted in him not being called in for any shifts for a long time.

Also working that night was David Warner, who had started a 24-hour shift on Sunday morning as pilot of the *Betelgeuse*.

The *Betelgeuse* with her crew of forty-two had berthed on the north side of the main jetty at Whiddy just after eight 'clock on the Saturday evening (6 January). She had in fact arrived in Bantry Bay two days previously but had to wait to berth, as her sister ship, the *Cassiopee*, had by coincidence arrived shortly before and then left on the Saturday afternoon, heading for Formosa. It was the *Cassiopee*'s last voyage; she was broken up for scrap after arriving at her destination.

Owned by Total, the French oil conglomerate, the *Betelgeuse* was built in 1968 when the trend was for developing ultra-large containers to transport crude oil because of the closing down of the Suez Canal during the Six Day War between Israel and Egypt in 1967. Voyages had become longer and it made more economic sense to carry as much crude oil as possible in one go.

As part of this new environment, Gulf Oil decided in the 1960s to search for a suitable site for a new terminal within reach of its European refineries and with a deep enough draft to accommodate the large tankers. Whiddy ticked all the boxes and, with the

Whiddy Oil Terminal

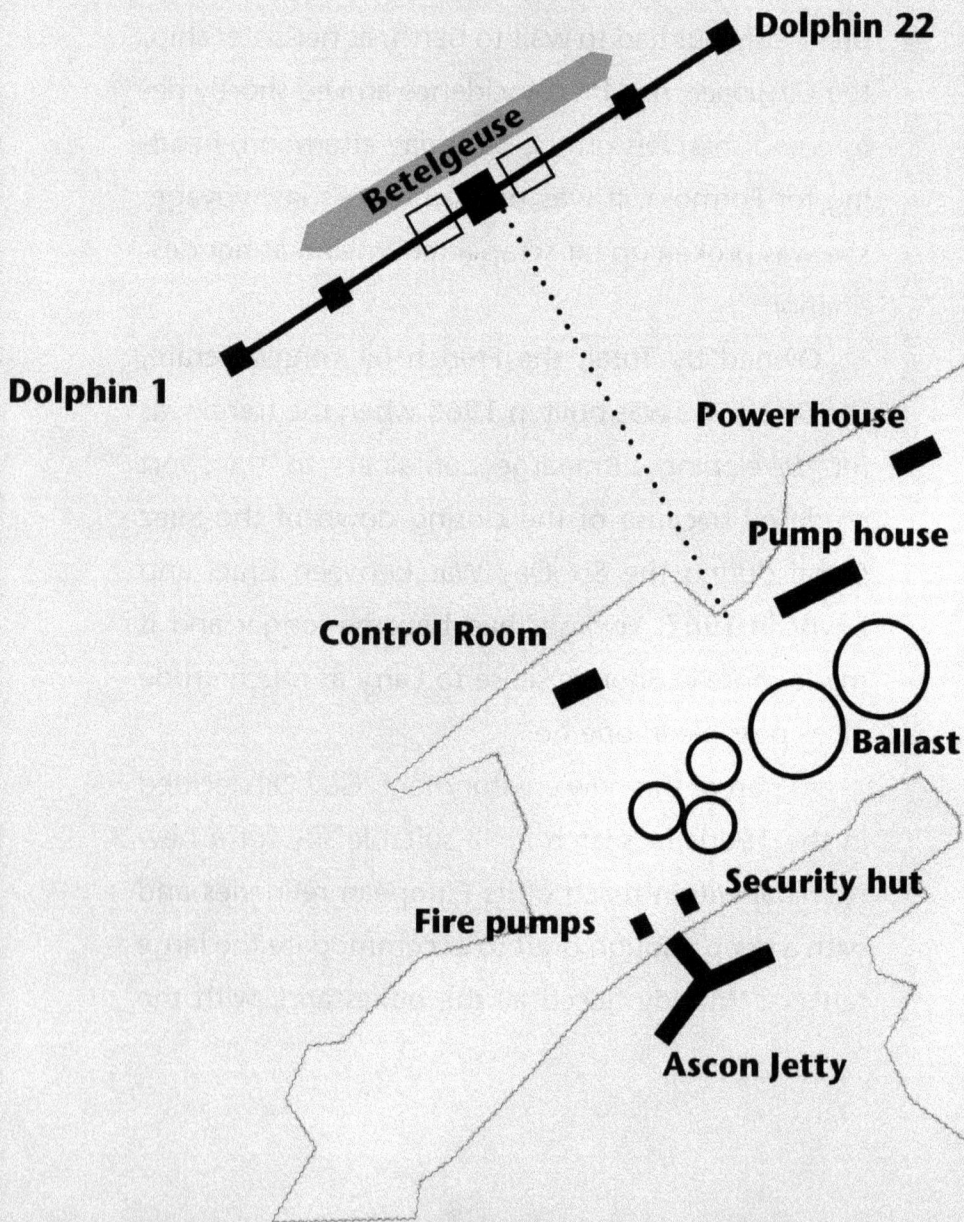

Dolphin 22

Betelgeuse

Dolphin 1

Power house

Pump house

Control Room

Ballast

Security hut

Fire pumps

Ascon Jetty

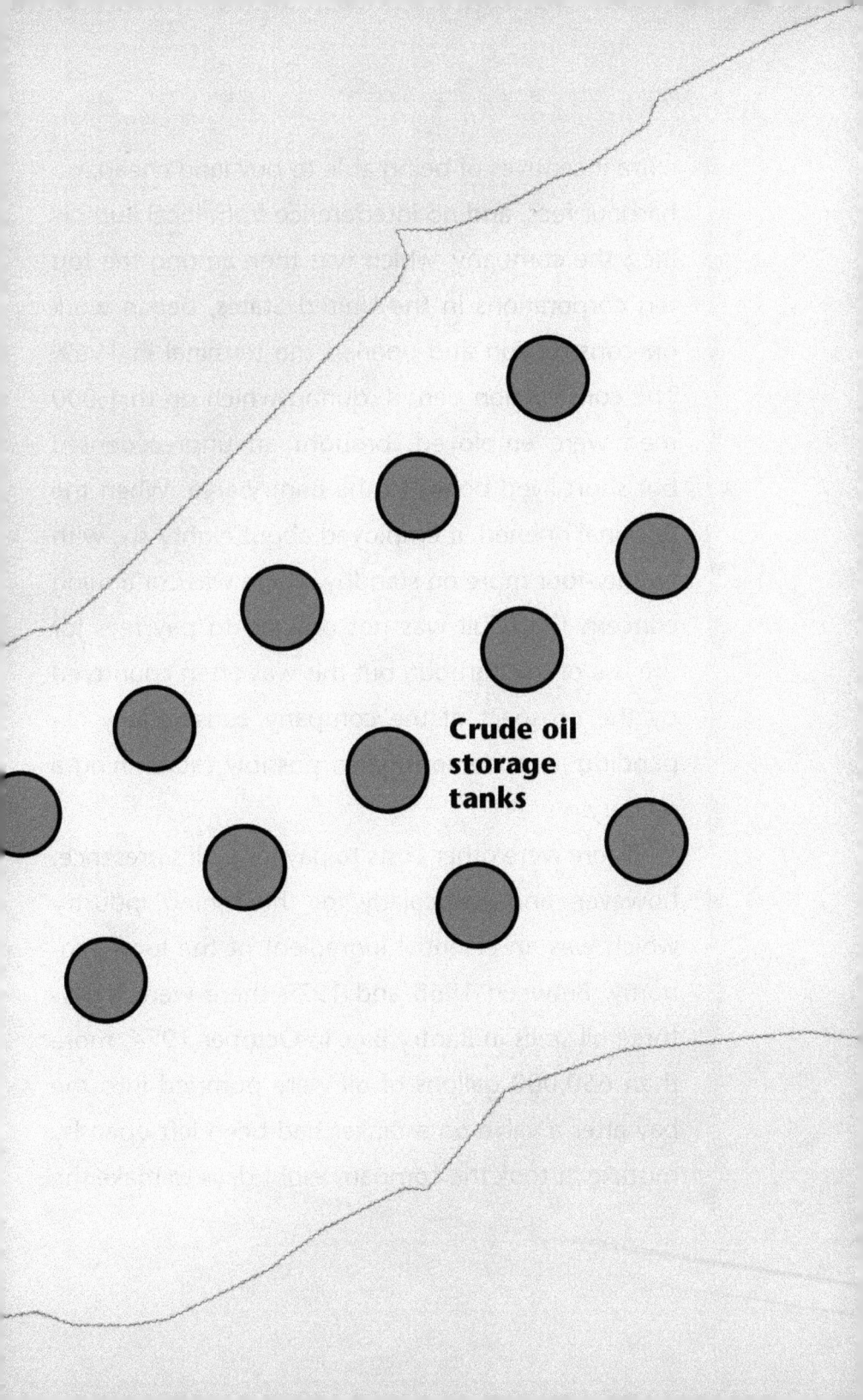
Crude oil storage tanks

extra incentives of being able to buy land cheap, no harbour fees, and no interference from local authorities, the company, which was then among the top ten corporations in the United States, began work on construction and opened the terminal in 1969. The construction period, during which up to 1,000 men were employed, brought an unprecedented but short-lived boom to the Bantry area. When the terminal opened, it employed about eighty-six, with twenty-four more on standby. There was continuing concern that Gulf was not obliged to pay fees for the use of the harbour, but this was often countered by the prospect of the company considerably expanding its operations, even possibly establishing a refinery.

There were other costs to pay for Gulf's presence, however, and particularly for the fishing industry which was an essential ingredient of the local economy. Between 1968 and 1979 there were thirty-three oil spills in Bantry Bay. In October 1974, more than 650,000 gallons of oil were pumped into the bay after a valve on a tanker had been left open by mistake. It took the company eight days to make the public aware of what had happened. More stringent precautions were put in place after this spillage but just two months later 115,230 gallons of crude oil spilled into the bay when a tugboat collided with a departing tanker. This led to the setting up of a harbour authority, but in reality it remained a toothless body.

By 1979, operations had been scaled down considerably at the terminal. The Suez Canal had opened again and an operation like that at Whiddy did not make as much economic sense as it had a few years previously.

The *Betelgeuse* had a length of just over 281 metres – slightly more than the length of two football pitches – and a deadweight tonnage (the weight a ship can safely carry) of 121,432 tonnes. She was certainly a big ship, but by no means the biggest to berth at Whiddy. This was the Gulf-owned *Universe Ireland*, which had been ceremoniously launched in Japan by Máirín Lynch, wife of Taoiseach Jack Lynch, in Japan in 1968. She the largest ship in the world at that time, with a deadweight of 312,000 tonnes and a length of 345.3 metres. The launching followed a

world-tour by the Lynches, and the fact that this had
been paid for by Gulf raised some eyebrows at the
time.

The *Betelgeuse* took up more than half the length
of the 488-metre-long jetty which lay 396 metres
from the shore. The jetty consisted of a series of is-
land-like structures on piles, groups of which formed
"dolphins", each with mooring facilities. The dolphins were connected by a catwalk. The dolphin
nearest to the open sea was Dolphin 1 and that
nearest to the head of the bay was Dolphin 22. The
latter contained a small hut for the security officer
and a coin-operated telephone kiosk with a direct
connection to the mainland. It was at this dolphin
that all jetty personnel and ship crews disembarked.
The dominant part of the jetty was the centre loading platform. This contained a personnel building,
the towering Chiksan arms used to connect tankers
to the submarine pipelines feeding the tank farm, as
well as the main fire-fighting system.

The terminal on the island covered 120 acres,
most of it taken up by the tank farm of twelve storage tanks, each with a capacity of 80,000 tonnes,

as well as smaller tanks for diesel, bunker oil, and ballast. Buildings included the power-house, the pump-house, the fire station, and the control office where all operations were co-ordinated and controlled. At the back of the terminal, where the view of the main jetty was blocked by a hill, was the Ascon jetty, where personnel disembarked. The three pumps feeding the fire-fighting system on the jetty were located here, as was the security hut.

Were it not for a shipping mishap in the Portuguese port of Leixoes, the *Betelgeuse* should never in fact have come to Bantry

The *Betelgeuse* began her voyage on 5 November 1978, leaving Leixoes, Portugal, for Ras Tanura in the Persian Gulf where on 24 November she took on her 120,00 tonnes of crude oil and then headed immediately for Europe via the Cape of Good Hope. On 26 December she arrived off Sines in Portugal where it was planned to discharge part of the cargo before proceeding to her final destination at Leixoes, where the remainder would be discharged. Bad weather, however, prevented her from entering Sines, and then the news came through that a ship had sunk across the entrance to Leixoes, blocking all entry. On 29 December, the captain received instructions from Total headquarters in Paris to proceed to Bantry after first stopping at Vigo to change some of the crew.

By six 'clock on the evening of 7 January, the *Betelgeuse* had discharged 77,098 tonnes of her 120,000 tonne cargo and then began the process of taking on ballast. While the discharge operation was in progress, the ship was visited by two survey-ors. Total had decided to sell the *Betelgeuse*, and the surveyors were there to give independent reports on her condition to two prospective buyers. One of the surveyors would later say that "it was a bloody awful looking ship on the day."

My duties that night took me as usual to different places around the terminal, at one point taking the Land Rover and driving up to the tank farm to carry out routine checks. The Land Rover was fairly clapped-out, and we always made sure to park it on a hill in order to make sure that we could start it, and more often than not we had to get it rolling first before the engine kicked in. After the tank inspections were done I headed back to the powerhouse office, where we always relaxed between jobs. Just before that, however, I dropped into the control room for a minute to give John Connolly a newspaper I was finished with before heading to the powerhouse where I was joined by Johnny Downey. At about thirty minutes after midnight Johnny went to check the generator while I continued to sit in the office. The powerhouse was completely sound-proofed, and if anything was happening outside, it would be impossible to hear it.

Not long after Johnny arrived back the telephone rang around 12.50am. It was John Connolly. The *Betelgeuse,* he said, was on fire. We ran out to the Land Rover, which thankfully started this time on first go, and I drove us both as fast as I could to the Ascon Jetty to check the fire pumps. At that stage, it appeared that there was only a small fire on the tanker. I was not really aware of it as I was concentrating on driving, but Johnny Downey would later say that it seemed to him that there was very little fire under the jetty's central platform; that the sea was on fire but not the jetty and the flames had not reached as high as the catwalk. He was sure that there would be "no problem" in getting people safely off the jetty. An explosion shook the air as we drove, but it was not of a force that caused us concern, nor was it anything like what would follow.

At the Ascon Jetty we checked that the fire pumps, which had already been started remotely by John Connolly in the control room, were operating properly. The two electric pumps were working, but the diesel pump was not. As we were inspecting the pumps, I saw the *Donemark* ferry leave to pick up the crew and others from the jetty. There was still no real sense of panic at this point, so we drove straight to the control room to get a clearer idea of the situation.

It was only then that we saw the full horror of what was happening.

The scene had changed utterly. Now everything seemed covered in fire, with flames jumping hundreds of feet. Just as I came in the door of the control room I heard Tim Kingston calling John Connolly over the radio for the *Donemark* to be sent out. He was told it was on its way, and then David Warner's voice broke in, saying that he was going to jump off the poop of the ship and wanted the boats to keep an eye out for him.

John Connolly asked Johnny Downey to make some phone calls as he was busy on the other telephone and the radio.

It was just at that point that I witnessed something that would burn itself into my memory until my dying day: a group of men running down the catwalk towards Dolphin 22 with flames swirling like a giant hand trying to engulf them. I knew in my heart that they were running in the wrong direction. The wind was coming from the west and blowing in the direction of Dolphin 22. They had no choice. Gulf had installed a gate at Dolphin 1, where there was a landing platform, but the gate was locked and surrounded with barbed wire, therefore not giving access to anyone heading for Dolphin 1. This area of the jetty remained untouched by the fire.

The gate to Dolphin 1 had been put in place by Gulf after an incident some years previously when a yacht had pulled up there and some unauthorized people had come on to the jetty. The company was keen to secure its property; perhaps it should also have given proper consideration to the safety of its workers. Gulf's fire officer had insisted that the key to the gate be held at Dolphin 22 in case of an emergency, but clearly the speed at which the fire had grown had made it impossible to retrieve this on the night. It would have been better if the key had been left with the jetty foreman, giving access to Dolphin 1 at all times, or if some sort of electronic security device had been installed on the gate.

The men on the jetty would have known that getting to Dolphin 1 would have greatly increased their chances of surviving. I can only imagine the horror they felt when they realised that this avenue of escape was completely barred to them.

As I saw the men heading for Dolphin 22, I knew that there was no hope of saving them. I had worked on the jetty for a good number of years and had plenty of experience of the ins and outs of everything there. Our fire training had instructed us always to get on the wind side of the fire to avoid the backlash of the flames blowing in your direction. Of the four Gulf employees on the jetty that night, three were relief workers, none of whom had been given full-time fire training, and the fourth person was a relief jetty foreman.

I turned to look at Johnny Downey who was trembling and overcome by shock as he gazed at the horrific sight in front of him. I caught him by his shoulders to shake him out of his shock and told him that we had to forget what was happening on the jetty and concentrate instead on protecting the rest of the island.

The building that was most immediately in danger was the powerhouse, which now had flames towering over it. And there was the even greater danger that the fire could spread quickly to the tank farm; if that happened, the consequences would be catastrophic for the whole island and Bantry itself.

As we left the control room to get fire-fighting equipment there was a massive explosion, the biggest of the many eruptions that would continue through the night. It shook us all to the core, and a total power failure followed immediately.

The sound of the explosion was heard throughout most of West Cork. People as far away as Ballinascarthy, about thirty-five miles as the crow flies, put it down to a violent thunderstorm in the west. A dinner dance at the West Lodge Hotel came to a halt when the floor began to tremble and the candelabras shake violently. Debris rained down on Bantry, but luckily did not cause serious damage. Small pieces of shrapnel landed in the Mealagh Valley, about six miles away.

In Glengarriff, about four miles directly across the bay, the heat following the explosion was felt quite noticeably and even some of the walls of the Eccles Hotel became distinctly hot. Some people bundled their families into cars and drove up to the hills for fear the fire would spread. The skies above Bantry were turned into an orange sheet that could be seen for miles around.

Fourteen families living on the island fled to the mainland in a flotilla of small boats. James O'Leary, whose house on Whiddy stood not far from the terminal, was alerted to the fire by his daughter. He went down to the shore to get a better view and was only there a few seconds when the main explosion occurred, followed by a huge ball of fire that jumped hundreds of feet in the air. Debris fell around him. He was stunned for a few minutes but then ran back to the house to get his family to leave.

Witnesses who saw the outbreak of the fire from the mainland said it seemed to be small at first — "the size of a motor car", according to one. It was confined to just forward of the centre of the *Betelgeuse* and was accompanied by sounds like distant thunder but then spread suddenly and dramatically along the whole length of the ship. After the explosion, witnesses heard continuous creaking and tearing noises.

It was crucial to get the power back following the explosion. Johnny Downey and I went straight to the powerhouse to restart the generator and then drove to the Ascon Jetty to recheck that the fire pumps were running. While there we picked up Jim Kearns and Pat O'Donnell, the two security men, and drove straight to the fire station.

To our horror, the fire-engine failed to start. We now had to lug the fire equipment in the clapped-out Land Rover. Johnny Downey dropped myself and

Pat O'Donnell off at the powerhouse to set up a water-cooling system.

There was already a jet fitted to the fire hydrant. I had great difficulty in opening the valve to the hydrant as the spanner I needed was in the fire engine at the fire station. When I finally opened the valve the nozzle blew off and took the helmet I was wearing with it. But I had no trouble finding it again and fitting it properly, as it was as bright as day from the flames.

I was now able to supply cooling water to the powerhouse. This was very important because the manifold was directly across from the powerhouse and was under severe heat, which could result in a build-up of pressure in these pipelines leading to the tanks. There were expansion joints on the pipelines which were designed for emergency pressure increase only. If the pressure wasn't relieved, the expansion joints would blow, resulting in a release of oil and gas, which would be highly dangerous, with naked flames towering over them and with shrapnel raining down from the explosions on the ship. Without the generator, John Connolly would not be able to open valves to relieve the pressure and prevent such a catastrophe.

I then went to Tank 5 to help Johnny Downey and Jim Kearns. It was a matter of urgency to protect this tank, which was closest to the fire.

When I go there I was shocked to see that all the fire hoses were brand new. I asked why they had brought up "those damn new hoses" when they hadn't been re-rolled and made ready for use. Johnny explained that we had already taken all the hoses out of the fire engine and these new hoses, which we weren't really aware of, were on the "ready-to-go rack" inside the main door, with the result that when they were opened they got all tangled up like a maze of extension leads.

I felt sorry for Johnny having to go down into the base of the tank single-handed and having to hold a high-pressure water hose to cool the tank. There was a big bank of earth around the tank to contain oil if the tank ever fractured, which made it more precarious.

Unfortunately they had brought up the old foam monitor, from which a manifold was missing to connect the hoses. "In the name of God why did you bring that thing up?" I shouted in exasperation. Johnny explained that the tow pin in the Land Rover would not fit the other canons because they were modified to connect to the fire engine tow bar only. That was all the more reason that the fire engine should have been in running condition. Gulf Oil claimed that it was out of commission as the foam tank was removed for repairs. Why weren't there other arrangements made to tow the fire canons?

I helped Johnny Downey and Jim Kearns to set up a single fire hose to the tank. Jim worked in security but had served for years in Bantry Fire Station.

When we were nearly ready we discovered there was no lever to open the hydrant. I told Jim Kearns to run as fast as possible to the next hydrant to see if there was a lever there and to keep going until he found something. Luckily, he came back quickly with one. We trained this single sad, sorry hose on Tank 5, and immediately steam rose off it in a terrifying manner.

As I was racing back to the fire station I was trying desperately to figure out how I could get something to use as a tow-pin for the proper cannon. As I was coming up to the T-junction between Tank 1 and Tank 6, the bonnet of the Land Rover flew up; it had been secured only with a flimsy stable bracket.

With all the explosions continuing around me and the blackness from the bonnet, I thought that Tank 5 had blown up and that I was gone. I never felt so fearful in all my life. When I got over the shock and discovered what had actually happened I realised that I had stopped only a few yards from the edge of the bank, barely escaping from going over and down on top of the pipelines.

I was trying to open the door of the jeep, but with all the panic it took me several seconds to remember that the lock on the door was broken and had been replaced with a shooting bolt similar to that of a garden shed. I pulled myself together, got back in the jeep and headed straight for the fire station. I now realised I could use one of the thin levers from the fire engine to use as a tow pin. Thinking the problem was solved, I then discovered that the legs supporting the fire canon had seized. I freed the legs by belting them with stones.

By that time the first person from the mainland had arrived to help. I was under severe pressure and he told me to calm down, but I don't think he realised how serious the situation was. Still, I was glad of the help and we immediately headed to Tank 5 to set up the water canon. By that time there were people appearing from everywhere.

On the mainland, Bantry Fire Brigade went on full alert and called on the assistance of the Skibbereen and Dunmanway brigades, but they were stranded on the pier for some time because no boat was available to transport them and their equipment. However, one member of the Bantry brigade, Michael Muckley, along with Billy Flynn, Gulf operations manager, did manage to get to the island on the Baltimore Bay.

Muckley went immediately to the workshop where he had to break a window to retrieve the keys for the three Land Rovers parked outside. He managed to start one of these after a number of attempts and drove to the fire station where he tried to activate the fire engine, but without success. After collecting all the hoses he could find with the help of Flynn, he brought these to the tank farm and then headed back to the Ascon Jetty to join the other members of the fire brigade who had just arrived. A further delay followed as there was no transport to bring the firemen and their equipment to the tank farm. When a truck eventually arrived and the equipment was loaded, it failed to start and had to be towed by Land Rover. The crews of the three brigades managed finally to get to the tank farm where they proceeded to help.

As well as having to deal with faulty equipment, we also lacked suitable clothing and equipment for fighting fires. There were no breathing masks or oxygen, nor did we have protective clothing. So immense was the heat (later estimated at 800 to 1,000 degrees centigrade near the burning wreck) that we had to spray ourselves with water in order to remain at the tanks. Battling the inferno for what seemed an eternity, I was filled with sheer dread, expecting at any moment that the tanks would overheat or be punctured and detonate, leaving Eleanor a widow and my little ones orphans.

We had to endure the heavy oily smoke and blasts of fierce heat with all the white-hot metal off the ship hissing through the air, thumping down all over the place. Any one of these fiery pieces could have ruptured the oil storage tanks and swept everyone away in an ocean of fire, including people in Bantry.

Rescue boats began to search the waters in the vain hope that some had swum to safety. The only vessels in the vicinity that could offer immediate help were the *Donemark* and the *Snave*, moored at the Ascon Jetty, and the Bantry Bay, a stand-by tug located south-east of Whiddy Point East. Neither the *Donemark* nor the *Snave*, however, had fire-fighting equipment and by the time they got to the jetty the whole area was swamped by fire. They did manage to get close to the bow of the *Betelgeuse* and Dolphin 1, but no crew member was able to get to this part of the ship, nor were any of those on the jetty able to get to Dolphin 1, which was unaffected by fire or the explosion, as access was blocked off.

Just as the major explosion erupted, the *Bantry*

Bay was approaching the jetty with fire pumps ready to spray foam. It found it impossible to get anyway near Dolphin 22 because of the heat and the flames. It was then instructed by John Connolly to give cover to the *Donemark,* and was able to get to within 100 feet of Dolphin 1, but there was no sign of survivors. Following another explosion it moved away and then was instructed to head to the Ascon Jetty to connect with the fire-main there. The skipper had considered pulling the *Betelgeuse* away from the jetty, but then realised that the bow was too high to do this and, in any case, it would have been impossible for anyone to climb up the dolphins to trip the quick-release mechanism to free the tanker from the jetty.

Despite all the difficulties we managed in the end to prevent the inferno from spreading. The list of equipment failures we had to contend with was mind-boggling. Within seconds of the fire alarm, we became aware that the diesel fire pump was out of service for maintenance. We were also appalled to find that the island's fire engine battery was flat, and the unit could not be started as the battery charger had not been plugged in. A second crucial diesel pump connected to the lake as a back-up pump didn't have any electrics connected to it and thus needed a hydraulic start. We continued to pump this until we were blue in the face, but it wouldn't start.

We only had two electric pumps to fight the fire and keep the cooling water sprayed on the generating station to ensure it kept operating. If we lost that we would have lost the island.

Incredibly, the metal support legs for the water cannon seized up, and I had to free them by hitting them with large stones. On top of that, fire-fighting equipment had to be dragged around the island in the Land Rover which was on its last legs with bad steering, poor brakes, and a clapped-out engine.

Despite all these setbacks we managed to keep the generator sheds free of fire and operating, thereby ensuring that disaster did not turn to catastrophe.

We knew we were not just fighting a fire. We were fighting for our lives.

The flames were lapping above the oil storage tanks, and the whole island was covered in burning chaff. We did not know if it was as a result of the burning oil, or debris of all manner and description raining down. At one point a huge chunk of metal, blown out of the *Betelgeuse* by the force of an explosion, soared like a missile through the air until it struck the earth close to Tank 1. The metal was white-hot, the size of a kitchen table and weighed over half a ton. If it had hit the tank or landed on top of the pipe-line, I don't think I would be here today.

Throughout that night I gasped for air, smothered in dense smoke and scorching fumes that scalded both throat and lungs and left a bitter taste in my mouth. My eyes were literally seared dry in their sockets and itched maddeningly. My exposed skin was stained everywhere with a black film of oil. I had no gear to protect my lungs or my eyes or skin from such a prolonged and intense exposure to the super-heated oil and other pollutants.

Fifty people died that night either as a direct result of the explosion or by drowning. Forty-two of the victims – including one woman who had gone on board with her husband, the ship's baker – were French, seven were Irish employees of Gulf, and one, a cargo inspector who had arrived at the jetty only minutes before the disaster, was English.

Just twenty-seven bodies were ever recovered. All but two were identified. On the Monday evening, about eighteen hours after the fire began, seven bodies were found on the north shore of the island and six in the vicinity of the jetty. The following day (Tuesday 9 January), when conditions had eased a little, a search party went out to Dolphin 22 and found the remains of eight bodies. Three of these were outside the security hut on the dolphin and five were inside. One of the bodies found outside was eventually identified as that of Liam Shanahan, one of the jetty utility men, but the other two were never identified. The five inside the hut were identified as members of the *Betelgeuse* crew.

Intensive searching continued over the following weeks. On 15 January, the body of Charles Brennan, a jetty utility man, was discovered on the eastern side of Dolphin 22, and some days later the body of James O'Sullivan, the stand-in jetty foreman, was found near the same spot. The remains of an inflatable life raft were discovered by Garda divers on

22 January and, about one foot away, the debris-covered remains of one the ship's petty officers. Following intermittent searches throughout February and early March, it was decided that the wreck had become too hazardous to continue searching, and all search operations were called off on 24 March.

On 19 August, the body of Cornelius O'Shea, the third jetty utility man, was discovered on the north shore of the island, and on the following day that of Tim Kingston, the pollution control officer, was found in the same location. On 1 November, the body of Denis O'Leary, the jetty security man, was also discovered on the north shore.

The post-mortem examinations revealed that the victims had died either from drowning or from "body tissue destruction, the result of exposure to explosive force and flame". Some of the bodies had been flung 500 yards away and were discovered beneath congealed oil on the shoreline.

The bodies of those who had drowned had also been damaged extensively by burning, but it was thought probable that this had happened after death. The the bodies of Cornelius O'Shea, Timothy

Kingston and Denis O'Leary had no signs of burning.

Later, the inquiry into the disaster would state that it could be assumed that some of those found on Dolphin 22 had been in their berths when the disaster occurred, and that some "significant interval of time" must have passed from when they were alerted to when they reached the dolphin. It also noted that all the bodies of crew members found in the water were more or less clothed, and it could be therefore assumed that they also had time to get dressed before jumping overboard to their deaths. It also believed that the evidence showed that there had been an attempt to make an escape from Dolphin 22 using the inflatable raft, but it could not be sure whether this had failed because of inadequate training of the jetty crew or because the raft was not in working order or because of the fire on the water.

According to the *Southern* Star of 20 January, a special Gulf report was expected to show that at least two of the tanks came close to exploding "in which eventuality a total holocaust could have enveloped the Bantry district, including perhaps even Glengarriff." It added: "While, as yet, no confirmed details have emanated from Gulf officials as to events at the scene, there is no doubt but that great gallantry must have been displayed by the two men [Brian McGee and Johnny Downey] who stood by their posts at the huge tanks and sprayed water continuously on them."

The *Betelgeuse* was split in two in the explosion. Both parts sank and 40,000 tonnes of crude were spilled. In some badly affected areas fishing was not possible and nets were damaged. Salvage operations continued for more than a year, in the course of which a Dutch diver met his death. The bow of the ship was removed first from the jetty and towed out to sea, where it was scuttled. The mid-section was then refloated and towed to Bilbao where it was scrapped. The stern was eventually brought to the surface in July 1980, placed on a pontoon and towed to Valencia in Spain where it was broken up.

The day after

ABOUT TEN O'CLOCK the following morning, with a black shroud of poisonous smoke still hanging over the island, I left for the mainland. The previous nine hours, in which I had little time to give much thought to myself, were now beginning to take their toll. Overcome by an exhaustion that seemed straight from the depths of hell, I felt confused and agitated and was hardly able to put two thoughts together, never mind explain to anybody what had happened. A whirlwind of sounds and images was raging though my mind, and at times I couldn't figure out if they were inside or outside of my head. I tried to slow everything down by holding onto one of the images, but as soon as I did it shot past to be replaced by another

Right then what I wanted most in the world was peace – the type of peace that only sleep could offer. But as much as I craved it, that most basic pleasure of deep, uninterrupted rest was to be denied me that day, and for many, many days to come.

I could not organize my thoughts. Although my body still moved and my mouth still formed words, somewhere deep beneath the surface, where my conscious had not yet registered it, the life of the father, the husband, the working man, and the human being that had been mine was no more. My own self, "Brian McGee", was dead.

When I eventually got back to Kealkill later that morning I didn't go home immediately but stumbled sobbing into the village church. I tried hard to pray, just to get a few words out, but my mind wouldn't let me. The images and noises still crashed about my head, and I felt ashamed for being alive. Eventually Eleanor found me and almost had to drag me up home, insisting that I try to get some sleep, but I couldn't lie down, much less close my eyes, and spent the day pacing back and forth throughout the house. It was the first bitter taste of the insomnia that would dog me for thirty years.

Someone from the Kealkill post office came to my house and asked me to phone John Lynam, the fire officer, as a matter of urgency. When I called him, he said that they needed "good strong men" to come to the terminal that night to help out with everything. He made the decision for me. I felt I had no choice; this was the job that had put bread on our table for the past ten years.

When I turned up that night the fire had subsided but the air was still thick with the acrid plume of smoke rising and spreading from the broken-backed *Betelgeuse*. The place that had become as familiar to me as the back of my hand now seemed so strange, so alien, as if the landscapes, faces, routines and reference points had been annihilated. Nothing seemed to have any meaning for me anymore.

Everyone who had been on duty the night before was ordered to write a detailed report about where they had been, what they had done, what happened when, and so on. We were also told that we had to do this on our own and not compare notes with anyone else. My stomach lurched when I heard this. Even at the best of times I found it difficult to put things on paper, but now with that whirlwind of sounds and images tearing through my confused mind such a task seemed impossible. Johnny Downey and I talked about this and it became clear that he felt the same, so we agreed that I would copy the details from the dispatcher's log in order to provide some sort of framework for our recollections of the night. The man who was standing in for the dispatcher saw me taking the information from the log but never said a word. I made an extra copy for Johnny Downey, but between one thing and another that night and because of my own confusion I forgot to give it to him while we were travelling home in the same car.

Some hours after finishing my shift Johnny arrived at my house to tell me that Gulf management had got a report that I had copied the log and were demanding that I return the copy. The management were accusing me of stealing the log; they believed that I wanted to sell it to the newspapers. Johnny said that I was to give the copies of the log to him and he was to hand them on to Seán Kearns, who was part of the management and also happened to be a brother-in-law of his. I refused, as I wanted to return the copies myself to Seán Kearns and explain why I had taken them in the first place. I also wanted to establish who had reported me. When I met Seán Kearns he point-blank refused to tell me that, but after a heated argument that threatened to turn violent he finally gave me the name on the understanding that I never divulge it, a promise I have kept to this day.

This was the beginning of a stormy relationship between me and Gulf management. And it was about to become even worse.

A few days later, Johnny, who had been talking to some people from *Frontline*, the RTE current affairs programme, approached me in the Bantry Bay Hotel and asked if I would agree to be interviewed along with him. I said no, but then after a few drinks allowed myself to be talked into it, and it was arranged that the interview would take place at eight o'clock that night in my house.

By the time the television crew had set up in my

sitting-room, there was no sign of Johnny. In hindsight, I should not have agreed to being interviewed on my own, but I had not slept for well over a day and I was not thinking straight about my own well-being and interests.

A controversy had arisen about when the fire actually started, and the interviewer pressed me to pinpoint a particular time, but I explained that I couldn't say for sure as I wasn't wearing a watch, and that in any case there were other things on my mind given the awfulness of the situation. I outlined where I was and what I had done on the night. I said that my only duty at the time was to try and make sure the fire didn't spread to the oil tanks, and that my mind was concentrated solely on this.

After the television crew had gone, Johnny arrived. He apologised, saying that he had fallen asleep. That may well have been the case, but I have often thought that the real reason was that he had second thoughts about being interviewed, perhaps after being warned by someone else. Whatever the reason, it was a wise move on his part.

The interview, just four and half minutes long, was

broadcast the following evening. The impact at work was immediate: I was ostracised first by management and then by practically everyone else in the following few weeks. It wasn't because I had said anything controversial. I had merely given a brief account of my own actions on the night, but the others obviously felt that I had broken rank. Behind every cold shoulder I received there seemed to lie the question, "Who do you think you are?" There was a lot of talk about the possibility of Gulf pulling out completely, and people were naturally concerned about the security of their jobs. The last thing they wanted was to think that one of their own had become something of a loose cannon.

For Gulf Oil, I certainly became an object of suspicion. The company would be the focus of any criminal or civil investigation to follow, and management became nervous about statements I might make and were no doubt trying to gauge how much of a liability I was.

For my part, I became extremely tense, convinced I was being closely watched for any slip-up on the job that would provide grounds for dismissal. I even became paranoid that I would be accused of doing something or failing to do something that would be highlighted as contributing to the disaster.

Some weeks after the disaster when I was back on my normal shift I called into the control room to find Don Ash, Gulf's top man in Bantry, there with some other people. He never acknowledged that I had come in or was even present. Johnny Downey was the control room operator that day, and Don Ash proceeded to praise him for the marvellous job he had done on the night of the fire. I felt hurt and embarrassed and I left the control room quickly. Outside, I waited for a while, wondering was I over-reacting, when I saw Don Ash come out to head up to the tank farm. I walked over to him but I had to step aside at the last moment to stop him bowling me over as he walked past brusquely as if I wasn't there. I knew then that I wasn't imaging what had happened in the control room.

For a while I continued to speak freely, both privately and publicly, about what I thought had gone wrong that night. Sleep continued to escape me, but I found my pain eased a bit when I spoke openly about what had happened. The more my torment was shared, the more it lessened. Word then got back to me that the management saw me as a threat, foolishly chattering away about things they felt were best left unsaid. I was being selfish, I was told, and that if I continued to speak out about the problems at Whiddy my big mouth would bring about the complete shut-down of the terminal. I would be held accountable for any job losses and would become so unpopular that my family and I would have to leave town.

The threats worked. There was no real choice but to go silent, bottling it all up and not speaking about it even to my family and friends. The misery became mine alone, and I faced each day, especially when I had to turn in for a twelve-hour shift, as if I had to push a heavy stone up a steep hill only to see it roll down to the bottom again. Everything seemed pointless. Time, I was told, would heal everything, and this was something I desperately wanted to believe. But then something else happened, and it was like suddenly falling off a cliff.

A few weeks after the disaster, I was on my own

around midnight in the powerhouse taking the generator log when I immediately sensed a presence behind me, a deeply evil presence that was threatening to engulf me. The fear that gripped me was like nothing I had never experienced before. My first instinct was to drop the clipboard I was holding and run as fast as I could. But the little bit of clear thinking I still had told me that I would have to face it. I turned around. There was nothing there, but the feeling of an overpowering evil still lingered.

My mind had plunged to a darker, more despairing level. From that night on I found myself extremely edgy and fearful on my own in the terminal. Sometimes a room I was in would become suddenly cold and I would hear what sounded like the buzzing of wasps in my ear. I hoped it was wasps, but it was winter, so it couldn't be. I would close my eyes to make out the sound and then it would become a jarring mix of individual voices talking and shouting angrily. I could never focus on one single voice. The words came too fast and tumbled over one another. And although I could never make out what they were saying, I was sure that they were trying to say something important. At other times, while walking through the terminal in the dark, I would sense people crowding close behind me, as if looking over my shoulder, but when I turned no one was ever there.

Another worker admitted to me one night that similar things had happened to him. He had spoken openly about it, but after he was ridiculed he decided he would keep his mouth shut. I decided to do the same.

Anyone who has gone through an overwhelming, terrifying experience is bound to suffer acute stress reaction after the event. And while most people manage to come to terms with what happened, with their symptoms of stress falling away steadily and then disappearing in a month or so, not everyone is so fortunate.

About one in three people, in fact, find it impossible to come to terms with what they have been through, and their symptoms continue unabated, sometimes for many years. This is the condition known as Post-traumatic Stress Disorder (PTSD), which under the term "shell shock" first came to recognition during the First World War and became the subject of intensive study and research in all subsequent major conflicts.

PTSD can start after any traumatic event, where one's life is threatened or where one sees other people dying or being injured, ranging from a serious accident or violent assault to a natural or man-made disaster. The more disturbing the experience, the more likely someone will develop PTSD. Research has shown that the most disturbing events are those that are man-made and unexpected and continue for a long time, causing many deaths, and are where someone is trapped and can't escape the horror of the situation.

One of the main symptoms of PTSD is the experience of re-living the event again and again, either as "flashbacks" during the day or nightmares when asleep. These can be so realistic that sufferers feel as though they are living through the experience all over again, and not just seeing it in their minds but sometimes also feeling the emotions and physical sensations of what happened – fear, smells, sounds.

Some sufferers may deal with the pain of their feelings by trying to feel nothing at all, by becoming emotionally numb, communicating less with other people who then find it difficult to live or work with them. Some people may also suffer from "hyper-vigilance", where they stay alert all the time, as if constantly on the outlook for danger. Such anxiety will make it very difficult for them to sleep, and they will come across as jumpy and irritable to those around them.

Depression also goes hand in hand with PTSD, along with physical symptoms such as muscle aches and pains, headaches, irregular heartbeats and diarrhoea. Panic attacks can become common, and sufferers will often seek relief in alcohol or drugs.

A number of explanations, both psychological and physical, have been put forward for why PTSD occurs, though much uncertainty remains. When someone is frightened, they remember things very clearly; although this can be distressing, it can help sufferers to understand what happened and, in the long run, help them to survive. On the physical side, the vivid memories may keep the levels of adrenaline in the body high, thus making a person irritable and unable to relax or sleep. Adrenaline may also affect the hippocampus, that part of the brain that processes memories. High levels of stress hormones can stop it from functioning properly, like "blowing a fuse". The flashbacks and nightmares continue because the memories cannot be processed as normal.

The night shifts on Whiddy became a time of prayer, begging for the angry voices to go away and not harm me. But then I began to wonder what use prayer was for the likes of me when those who had died had probably called on God for help, but to no avail. I began to have as many as possible Masses said for the souls of the dead, until finally the priest at Kealkill told me to stop. "Enough is enough," he said. Without their Masses, I thought the dead could never be satisfied, would never allow me to have peace anywhere, be it at work, at home or in the church.

In trying to overcome PTSD, sufferers can often meet a number of barriers put up by other people. They may not let a sufferer talk about what has happened and may go out of their way to avoid them. They may even become angry with the sufferer or think of them as weak or even blame them. All of this only helps to isolate the sufferer further in their pain.

Up to that point in my life I had been a normal social drinker – a few pints in the local pub for a bit of "craic" with the mates, and home. And then whiskey arrived with a solution. It seemed to be the only thing that could numb the pain or smother the screams that wanted to get out of me, and I began to drink it heavily. But, welcome as this temporary relief was, it was really only adding fuel to the fire. My family began to suffer awfully. We had always been fairly close and they were now trying their best to cope with me, but they really had no hope of understanding what I was going though, nor could I explain it to them. I shouted and roared at them for no reason. Things that had never bothered me before now brought down a red mist of anger. Unable to sleep, I would pace about for hours and often leave the house so as not to keep my family awake, driving or walking the roads, then returning with no memory of where I had been or what I had done. It was hard enough walking the roads, as my physical health had also started to deteriorate rapidly, and my feet had started to bleed.

It was not the fault of my family that I was acting like a madman. They had not changed, I had; they were normal, I was not. They were gentle and supportive, but even this I found galling. In a perverted way their normality irritated me no end and their innocent ignorance was infuriating. My sleeplessness became steadily worse; many times I would manage to get just one hour of fitful rest in a day.

Some other strange things began to happen. Except for two nightmares that continued to haunt me for years after the disaster, I cannot remember any dream or nightmare that had the least splash of colour in it. It wasn't just that I lost interest in colour; I didn't even notice it, not the flowers, not the trees, not the sky above, not even the shirt on my back. And then I lost my sense of smell, except for two things: oil and ash.

The smell of oil still turns my stomach, and it reminds me of what was in the air that night and how some of it along with the steady downpour of ash must have lodged in my lungs.

In one of the two nightmares that regularly visited me I used to see the lads running from the flames and me running towards them to help them, but then I am either trapped in the flames or I am outside them trying to get in. I could never tell how long the nightmare lasted, but it seemed an eternity, and when I awoke it felt as if I was on fire and I would be drenched in sweat.

The second nightmare would start pleasantly, as if I was out enjoying myself. There always seemed to be a lot of people around, as if there was a celebration of some kind. Then it would suddenly switch to a beautiful woman coming into the bedroom, whom I would greet with open arms. To my horror, she would then turn into a completely evil monster, and I found myself being clamped to the bed by her. Her head would then go into a pointed shape and as she got closer her eyes appeared to be burning through me. It seemed as if she was trying to get into my mouth and down my throat as if to steal my very soul. It was only when I was able to get the Saviour's name, Jesus, out that the whole nightmare began to evaporate.

One night I woke up to become aware of a huge black presence at the end of my bed. I got up to confront it, using the Lord's name to rid me of this evil. As I moved closer, it moved away and I could hear the floor boards creaking. I followed it though the rest of the house, which had concrete floors, but I could still hear the creaking. Eventually it left me. In some strange way this did not affect my mental condition, or at least make it worse; in fact, overcoming this evil presence strengthened my faith.

My experience of time itself seemed strange: sometimes speeding up, sometimes suspended, and moving backwards and forwards or altogether lost. The internal rhythm I had lived by for thirty-two years was all out of kilter.

Most people at first tolerated my mood swings, but in time their patience began to wear thin. "Put it all behind you" was a frequent bit of advice, as was "Get on with your life" or "Give thanks you were spared." Some recommended that I pray to this or that saint or try this or that novena, or wear this or that medal. They meant well, but it was often like having salt rubbed into my wounds, and although I tried my best, nothing worked. Anyone who really knew me from before the disaster were painfully aware that something was no longer quite right about me, that I had become a different man. As for me, I thought everyone else had changed. I was too far gone to see how truly unstable I was becoming.

The Tribunal

While smoke still billowed from the *Betelgeuse*, Gulf Oil began to face a barrage of questions from the media about the possible cause of the disaster, in particular about what time exactly the fire had started and why it had not been possible to rescue anyone on the ship or jetty.

It also became quickly clear that the company had decided to go into defensive mode, just as it had when major oil spillages in 1974 and 1975 had polluted the bay. In July 1980 the *Sunday Independent* published details of what it described as "a top secret document" which gave clear guidelines to

Gulf executives about how they should deal with media enquiries about the disaster. The objective, it said, was "to cushion any unfavourable impact of disaster incidents such as oil pillages and fires." The executives were warned not to discuss a wide range of topics with anyone outside the company, including the cause of the disaster, estimates of property damage, compensation, and the cost of the clean-up operation. They were also warned to be aware of journalists who might ask pertinent questions: "Don't be stung by barbs. Throw charges right back at the one who hurled them, otherwise it may appear that there is no defence."

In 1987, Michael Regester, who was Gulf's public relations man assigned to "manage" the fall-out from the disaster, published a book titled *Crisis Management: How to Turn a Crisis into an Opportunity* in which he described, in a chapter headed "Bad Day at Bantry Bay", how the company was able to neutralise the media onslaught in the days following the disaster. Journalists were clamouring for a press conference at which they could question John Connolly directly about when the fire started and whether he had reacted quickly enough, or at least to have a signed statement from him. Under clear instructions from Gulf management, Michael Regester refused to issue any such statement or to grant access to John Connolly, citing legal reasons and the possibility of prejudicing any subsequent inquiry.

The most crucial question that journalists wanted to ask Connolly directly was about when he became aware of the fire. Right from the start, Gulf insisted that it had begun at 12.55am, and that the controller had acted promptly and responsibly. This time, however, was in clear contradiction to what had been reported by a significant number of eye-witnesses. A number of newspapers, for instance, had reported that two gardai on duty that night had seen the fire at 12.30am, but this turned out to be erroneous as a result of the confusion that prevailed in the immediate aftermath of the tragedy and was later corrected to 12.45am, which was still significantly different from what Gulf maintained. Gulf would later try to use this discrepancy to have the gardais' evidence discounted as false, but this was unsuccessful.

The anger over this refusal, or indeed over the

company's reluctance to address directly any questions about what had happened on the night, was well caught in an editorial in *The Southern Star* of 20 January, which said that it could not "be in the interests of anybody, least of all Gulf, to pursue a policy of deliberately withholding vital information from the press and public and prevent essential witnesses such as Mr. John Connolly from being interviewed." It added that no company, multinational or not, could claim "to 'own' the lives of the workers it employs and this, in a sense, appears to be the philosophy behind the 'privileged information' line being put out by Gulf spokesman."

According to Michael Regester in his book, for a few days media hostility towards Gulf "escalated to an unbelievable level – so much so, that it became very difficult for me to persuade senior Gulf people to attend press conferences at all."

Eventually, however, Gulf managed to defuse the situation, without producing John Connolly, by fielding technical staff at the conferences who could report on the progress being made on the salvage and pollution clean-up operation. "In other words,"

Michael Regester wrote, "we began making our own news" – thus diverting journalists' attention away from their original line of questioning.

Michael Regester severed his links with Gulf not long after and went on to become a highly success-ful international consultant on crisis management. In November 2008, in an interview with *The Na-tional*, an English language newspaper in Abu Dh-abi, he stressed the importance for a company to tell the truth in the event of a crisis and remarked about his experience at Bantry: "I can honestly say I made every mistake it was conceivable to make. My biggest mistake was to believe the lawyers. They lied to me, so I unintentionally lied to the press, and a few months later it all came out."

The Gardai, as required by law, carried out their own investigation of the disaster, during the course of which it became clear that Gulf management were not only not prepared to budge from their ver-sion of events but were not even prepared, in the interests of establishing the truth, to consider the overwhelming amount of contrary evidence from other sources. Even with full cooperation from Gulf, which there patently was not, a Garda investigation into such an immense tragedy was bound to be limited, and it was quickly realised by the public and politicians that a judicial tribunal of inquiry would have to be established. Accordingly, after some debate in the Dáil, the government in March set up the inquiry which it also decided, after persistent representations from West Cork deputies, would be held in Bantry. Appointed to head the inquiry was Declan Costello , a High Court judge who had been a prominent Fine Gael deputy and son of John A Costello, the former Taoiseach. The inquiry held its first sitting in the West Lodge Hotel in Bantry on 26 April 1979. It would sit for seventy-two days, hearing evidence from 184 witnesses and submissions from twenty-three barristers. It would deliver its findings to the government on 9 May the following year.

My reaction to the news of the setting up of the tribunal was mixed. On one hand, I had a feeling of hope that the state, in the course of establishing the truth, would somehow find a way to protect me and make matters right. Just as they had a duty to the dead and their families to find out what had happened, the authorities, I thought, would also out of a sense of justice show practical compassion for those whose lives had been put at risk and had suffered in other ways.

This vague sense of hope, however, was overridden by a deep anxiety about the tribunal itself, adding another layer of mental anguish. I knew I would be called as a witness, and this posed a number of problems. As someone who had left school at 14 and was not well-read, I was worried how I would handle myself in a room full of lawyers and journalists. What if I was asked a question and did not understand some of the words? What if I couldn't find the right words to explain something? Would I be able to hold myself together in the witness stand and not break down? These self-preoccupied thoughts were a product of my mental state at the time, and as the first sitting of the tribunal approached, they grew worse. It was if a legal juggernaut was rumbling its way towards Bantry and would crush any little bit of pride I had left.

There was also the problem of what I would be

asked and what I would tell the tribunal. There was a lot swirling around in my mind about what I knew about operations at the terminal and the various short-cuts the company had taken.

There were just so many things wrong on Whiddy you could fill a book with them if you took a mind to make a list, which nobody ever cared to do from the time I first started there. There was trouble with the electrics, the safety gear, the jeep, and the fire-fighting equipment. There was something always going wrong or waiting to go wrong. If anything was brought to the attention of management, promises would be made, but in reality everything was put on the long finger. In truth, nobody ever wanted to make a fuss, for there was always the fear at the back of everyone's minds that Gulf could just pack up and leave, which was an understandable fear to some extent because of the way the company had been cutting back on operations at the terminal for a number of years. The threat of closure always seemed to be hanging in the air. I remember how in the early part of 1979, when celebrations were held to mark the tenth anniversary of the terminal, Bill Finnegan, the head of Gulf in

Ireland, was interviewed on RTE and refused outright to give any assurance that operations would continue in Bantry. That, of course, only helped to increase people's fears about the future. (Incidentally, I also remember, that part of the celebrations involved an extensive demonstration of fire-fighting procedures in front of invited guests and the RTE cameras, but this had to be cut short because the foam system on the tug failed to work.)

It was written into the company procedure that the equipment to be used in the event of a fire was checked to ensure it was fit for its purpose. The person responsible for carrying out the checks had a list which they ticked off or, in the case of non-compliance, wrote a comment against the relevant piece of equipment. This was done at the end of the day's shift. On the day before the disaster, Teddy Cronin, an assistant pump man like myself, carried out the check and wrote a comment on the list that Diesel Fire Pump 409 was out of order.

Following the disaster, the operations manager made a statement that according to his records the check of the fire-fighting equipment had not been

carried out. This was strongly denied by Teddy Cronin, who had two years' experience of working in the terminal fire station and was fully aware of the consequences if any non-compliance was not reported.

The checklist that he filed was "lost", which raises quite a number of questions. Would Gulf not have wanted to show that list to demonstrate how careful they were about safety? Should the tribunal not have demanded to see it? Teddy Cronin was told that he would not be called as a witness in the tribunal. It was a strange decision, considering his part in operations at the terminal.

Gulf, which had been severely criticised on a number of occasions for causing oil spillages, were always keen to promote themselves as a company that was committed to the environment and to the safety of its workers. The window of its Bantry office displayed a number of trophies that a number of us had won in various fire-fighting competitions. Immediately after the disaster these were removed. Why? Was it that the company did not wish the world to know any longer that its workers were highly proficient when it came to safety matters, thus leaving the door open to laying the blame for the shortcomings on the night on human failure rather than on faulty equipment and poorly devised procedures?

About three weeks before the tribunal began I approached the Gulf Oil general manager, Don Ash, calling into his office unannounced. His first reaction was to tell me that he was a very busy man and had no time to talk to me, but then backed down when he saw how determined I was. I felt strongly that someone in his position should be made fully aware of the poor state of the fire equipment on Whiddy. After he listened to what I had to say he called in Billy Flynn, the operations manager, and asked me to repeat what I had told him. Flynn, however, would not accept any of what I had to say and proceeded to make excuses for the fire safety officers. I made it quite clear that I was not going to tell lies or cover up in any way for the negligence of the company. Don Ash's last words to me were: "If you tell that in the stand at the tribunal you will be the cause of closing down the oil terminal and people will lose their jobs. And if you think you had trouble before, you'll have a lot more now."

When it came to my turn to give evidence at the tribunal I was in a terrible state physically and mentally, but I got through it with the help of tablets from my doctor. I didn't give more than was asked of me and I didn't volunteer information that wasn't looked for. When it was over I was disgusted with myself. I had kept my peace but, the truth be told, I hated myself for not grabbing the chance to set things right in front of everybody. It would have been difficult to cut through the lawyers who seemed to object to everything that came out of people's mouths, but I regret to this day that I did not take the opportunity to not put the record straight about the mess that Whiddy had been in for years and highlight the fact that no government official had ever bothered to give the terminal a close look. I cannot be certain, but perhaps it would have made some difference.

One day during a break in the hearings, which were held at the West Lodge Hotel, I was in the bar with a few others when I became aware of some lawyers standing nearby chatting and laughing with each other. One of them, rubbing his hands together, said quite audibly, "Now we got them!" At that point John Connolly was on the stand – a man who in my opinion was unjustly used as a scapegoat for the disaster – and it made me sick to think that they saw it all as some sort of game. I was hoping to hear what else they had to say, but Jim Kearns who was with me made some remark that made it clear who we were, and the lawyers clammed up and then left as soon as possible.

It made me sick to see that certain people never got called to the stand. Other people from Gulf should have been up there, people who knew a lot about the sorry state of Whiddy before the disaster. No doubt it would have been legal suicide for Gulf to call them, but it was very strange to me that the government never did. All they had got was one witness who was totally confused and bamboozled, which to me seemed a long way from any desire to establish the truth and achieve justice.

As the inquiry progressed my frustration grew deeper as it became clear to me that the right questions about Whiddy were not being asked – questions that should have been raised by those in the tribunal, but were not. And it was also clear that the spotlight was not being diverted from one interested party, the government, which had clearly failed in its duty to monitor the situation at Whiddy.

There was too much left unsaid and unanswered, and some employees who worked the day shift, including the jetty foreman, should have been called to give evidence but appear to have got lost along the way. Since the downturn at Whiddy the utility men were removed from the jetty to do maintenance work on the tanks, but the jetty foreman remained on the jetty as caretaker, so anyone in that position would have been very knowledgeable about all aspects of safety and the equipment used. I therefore can't help but ask why the jetty foreman on the day shift before the disaster was not put on the stand. He was someone I had helped to train into his job, and the only conclusion I could come to about him not being called was that Gulf management knew that he would be a poor witness for them. The simple fact was that Gulf Oil decided who was going to give evidence, which in my mind brought into question the independence of the tribunal. It seemed to me that there were so many questions that were left unasked. I could never understand, for instance, why the tug had not sprayed foam to dampen the fire on the *Betelgeuse*. Is it possible that the foam system was not working? I don't recall this being ever raised. Also, in the early days there was a jockey pump, the function of which was to keep the fire main charged at all times. However, it began to cause some problems, and Gulf's way of addressing these was to remove it and dump it behind the powerhouse. This was never mentioned.

My misgivings about the conduct of the inquiry were confirmed some months into the hearings when Kenneth Hugh Black, an expert adviser, resigned from the tribunal, saying he was unable to carry out the task for which he had been appointed". That someone so close to the inner workings of the tribunal was forced to take this action raises a lot of questions about the way the whole investigation was being carried out.

Dr Hugh Kenneth Black, from England, was one of three experts appointed as assessors to the tribunal.

He had served as chief inspector of explosives for the British Home Office and was highly regarded as an international expert on dangerous substances. In October 1979, after tending his resignation to Judge Costello, he issued a highly critical statement to the press, explaining that he had resigned for two reasons: "Firstly, I had never heard such evidence as was given by some witnesses, and, secondly, restrictions were imposed on me in questioning others. I was unable, therefore, to carry out the task for which I was appointed."

Dr Black went on to say that some witnesses had been released without the most important questions being put to them and consequently the answers to these questions were now lost to the tribunal. He had been "greatly distressed" that he was unable to pursue his inquiries.

He listed a number of points that he felt should have been raised:

- The design of the terminal was fundamentally wrong, as there were no sufficient safeguards in relation to operations, fire-fighting and the evacuation of personnel.

- The fire equipment and fire-fighting arrangements, ashore and on the platform, were such as to make it imperative to close down until the defects were remedied.

- The emergency evacuation of personnel had not been seriously considered, nor had recent training taken place.

- The arrangements for dealing with fires on the jetty were ludicrous, as the fire mains could only started from the control room ashore.

- The platform crew had no means of fighting the fire, nor were there any means whereby they could be rescued and they could not help themselves, because he doubt very much whether anyone knew how to use the life-raft on Dolphin 22, or had even seen it demonstrated. The company was "living in a fool's paradise" if it thought that a life-raft would be of any significant help other than in ideal weather conditions, and probably in day time.

"There is no need for me to go into the serious

deficiencies of the Manuals," Dr Black added, "or to comment on the devastating electrical and mechanical reports on the jetty, nor need I refer to the management or to the lack of local or central government control, for I have already said enough to indicate that there was a very great deal wrong on the ship, and ashore."

He also had something to say about the role of John Connolly. "In regard to the dispatcher, he worked a twelve-hour shift and alone. He was the key man, the linchpin, on whom everything depended in the event of an accident. I do not believe that any man can remain fully alert during such a period, particularly at night. No man should be expected to work such long hours and to shoulder alone the enormous responsibility that the dispatcher had to bear. It is a very grave reflection on the company that they expected him to do so."

Dr Black ended his statement by saying that he could "only speculate on the reasons that prevented me from making a full inquiry into the aspects that were of the greatest importance." He only knew one way of inquiring into serious accidents, and that was to pursue the truth fairly and honestly without fear and without favour to anyone.

"It was an accident that should never have been allowed to happen but, having occurred, there should have existed, and there could have existed, plans and arrangements whereby some, if not all personnel, could have been saved.

"An enormous amount of work will need to be done if ever the terminal is reconstituted, in order to put it into a satisfactory basis. Harbour bye-laws will need to be promulgated, a code of practice set up, and entirely revised operations and disaster manuals and personnel fully trained in petroleum technology.

"It will be essential to exercise expert central government control and inspection."

The full text of Dr Black's statement is given in an appendix to this book.

For me, Dr Black had put his finger on the issues that mattered most, but particularly on what should have been an important focus of the tribunal, but wasn't, and that was the role of the government, which had left Gulf to its own devices and had failed totally in its duty to monitor the situation on Whiddy. But it was clear from the proceedings that this was something that was going to be side-stepped.

The findings of the inquiry report were published in July 1980. The report made difficult reading.

The tribunal findings

THE MOST DISTURBING aspect of the tribunal report for me and many others was the way it pointed the finger directly at John Connolly – in effect turning him, with the help of a media that wasn't really looking in the right place or asking the right questions, into a scapegoat. As well as being unjust, this directed attention away from where it should have been: the careless way in which Gulf had from the very beginning approached safety and fire-fighting standards and – what was just as bad, if not worse – the total failure by the politicians to bring in regulations to ensure that those standards were met in the first place. Politicians claim to make decisions for the benefit of us all. In this case, either because of their short-sightedness or just plain lack of interest, they failed to live up to their responsibilities, with a tragic result for so many. And, as so often happens, no one was ever called to account for this negligence or had to pay the least price.

> The tribunal findings, published on 9 May 1980, were quite clear that the huge loss of life on the night could have been avoided if it had not been for the negligence displayed by three parties: Total, Gulf Oil, and the public authorities.
>
> Total's neglect of the *Betelgeuse*, it found, had been the initial cause of the fire and subsequent explosion, but the nature of Gulf's response to the outbreak along with poor safety and emergency procedures had prevented at least some, if not all, of the crew and jetty workers being saved.
>
> The tribunal was also critical of the government for its failure to put in place regulations that would ensure that proper safety and emergency procedures were adhered to by Gulf; this was an aspect of the

findings that did not at the time receive the media attention and analysis it deserved, being swamped by the more dramatic headlines about John Connolly and other Gulf Oil personnel generated by the report.

The findings dismissed out of hand Total's claim that the fire had started on the jetty – possibly even as a result of someone smoking there – and had then spread to the *Betelgeuse*. The technical evidence and the statements of eye-witnesses, according to the tribunal, had clearly established clearly that the source of the initial fire was on the ship, and this was corroborated by the fact that some crew members had escaped from the ship to seek safety on the jetty, which they were unlikely to have done if there was a fire there.

The primary cause of the fire was the collapsing of the ship's hull because of an incorrect ballasting operation, following which vapour from empty ballast tanks escaped into the vessel and erupted into a fireball. The collapse of the hull would not have happened, the inquiry determined, if the *Betelgeuse* had been properly maintained or if she had been fitted with an inexpensive piece of equipment known as a "loadicator", which would have alerted those in command of potentially dangerous sagging in the structure. Total, however, had long neglected the *Betelgeuse*, seeing little financial sense in continuing to invest in a hard-worked, 11-year-old ship that it was planning to sell, possibly for scrap. The vessel was badly corroded, and parts of her structure were badly wasted so that the stresses set up during un-loading and ballasting were well above the critical limit, leading to a weakening of the deck and side plating, which in turn buckled to cause a progressive failure of the hull.

Whatever the source of the fire (and Total, it must be noted, has never accepted the tribunal's conclu-sion on this matter), it was the response to the out-break and the emergency procedures put in place by Gulf that received the most attention in the findings.

The fire-fighting system originally in place at the terminal was, in the judgement of the tribunal, "of good international standard", but modifications over the years had the effect of down-grading it. For instance, management had decided just a few years after operations began not to keep the fire-mains pressurised, which meant that the jetty crew could not activate the system without the intervention of the dispatcher in the control room; in the eyes of the tribunal, it was a short-sighted decision, taken without an adequate appreciation of its consequences. If this decision had not been taken, it was possible (though, the report admits, not certain) that the jetty crew might have been able to contain the fire.

The findings also noted that important fire-fighting equipment had been allowed to remain inoperable much longer than desirable. Standards of maintenance had fallen for some time before the disaster because of "economy measures and not through lack of skill or dedication by the maintenance personnel."

There had been an equal decline in safety standards. Employees who worked on a temporary basis had not received any formal training in fire-fighting techniques, but what was of greater consequence was the fact that no escape plan had been formalised. With a proper plan in place, along with a proper supply of escape craft and access to Dolphin 1, it was "possible . . . that the lives of most of the jetty crew would have been saved."

Another major defect in the emergency procedures stemmed from a management decision to allow the duty tug to moor at a considerable distance from, and out of sight of, the jetty – a significant change in practice made some years previously. If the tug had been kept close to the jetty, the report said, "the lives of the jetty crew and those on board the vessel would have been saved", and it was even possible that the fire could have been contained to the *Betelgeuse*. As it was, the *Bantry Bay*, the tug on duty on the night of the disaster, which was equipped with high-capacity fire-fighting equipment, was moored nearly three miles away from the jetty and at a point where it was out of sight of the jetty; it would have taken it twenty minutes to arrive at the scene of the fire.

The main brunt of the tribunal's criticisms, however – and the one that the media concentrated on – concerned the role of John Connolly. The tribunal was quite adamant that he was not in the control room to see the fire begin, that he tried to cover this up by insisting that the fire had started at 12.55am, much later than the time given by other witnesses, and that a number of Gulf personnel had taken "active steps" to suppress the truth about really had happened.

It was clear well before the tribunal hearings started that Gulf's unwavering insistence that the fire had started at 12.55am was going to be seriously challenged. Much of the media coverage immediately following the disaster had highlighted the disparity between this claim and the times given by other eye-witnesses, including two gardai, which was the reason there was such a clamour for John Connolly to be interviewed, a request that Gulf doggedly resisted. Gulf's reluctance to even consider the possibility that it was wrong about the time was starkly illustrated at one point in the hearings when Don Ash, the manager of the terminal, was asked to comment on the earlier times given by some eye-witnesses. "I think that is total nonsense," he said. He also dismissed the reports in the press about the other earlier times that had been given as being merely "allegations" that were "completely false."

Was the 12.55am time given by John Connolly one that he completely believed in himself? Or was it one that Gulf management, for their own ends, insisted that he maintain through thick and thin despite all the contrary evidence from other witnesses?

The part of the tribunal report dealing with the interview he gave as part of the Garda investigation hints at on a possible answer to those questions, and also throws some light on his relationship with management, and its underlying tensions, in the run-up to the tribunal.

On 15 January, after being contacted by Garda Patrick Joy he came to the Garda Station that afternoon in the company of Joseph Smith, Gulf's American lawyer. The report noted a "striking difference in evidence" as to how it came about that Smith accompanied him. According to John Connolly it was the result of a casual meeting while he was on his way to the station; according to Smith, it had been arranged earlier that morning between them that he would accompany him. For the tribunal, Smith's evidence was "obviously the correct account", a sure indication of the poor standing in which it regarded John Connolly as a witness. The real significance of this, however, is that it shows how Connolly was probably unhappy with the undue, almost claustrophobic, attention he was receiving from his superiors and wanted to establish some distance between him and them, that he wanted somehow to dispel the view that he was being controlled by his masters.

What happened subsequently at the station is also revealing and probably provides a brief but real glimpse into what John Connolly knew happened that night. Watched carefully by Smith and answering questions by Detective Garda Patrick Hogan, he completed his statement over the course of four hours. At one point he stated that "to the best of my knowledge the *Donemark* must have left Bantry Pier at about twelve midnight as I remember well the *Donemark* passing my window and docking at Dolphin 22 at 12.20 am." The significance of this is that with this time, and not the 12.40am arrival time being given by Gulf management, it was clear that the fire could have started earlier than they maintained. Smith immediately jumped in and said, "John, this is not what you told me. You cannot say what time the *Donemark* left Bantry Pier. You are only surmising." Garda Joy then remonstrated with Smith, saying that he was not entitled to intervene but could only take notes, to which Smith replied, "It doesn't matter anyway, you will never prove what time the *Donemark* docked at Dolphin 22 as the log is burned" – referring to the security log that had been at Dolphin 22. Despite Smith's objection, the 12.20am time of arrival was kept in the statement, which Connolly then signed after agreeing with the gardai that it was a true account of what had happened. This was against the advice of Smith who said, "There are a couple of things that will not stand up in court."

In his oral testimony to the tribunal, however, Connolly stated that his statement to the Gardai was incorrect and that he could not have said that the *Donemark* had arrived at Dolphin 22 at 12.20am. On this, the report noted that in the mind of the tribunal his original statement had been properly taken and accurately recorded what he had said. It also noted that Connolly had not complained that he was in any way put under pressure by the gardai to change his evidence in any way, and that if he had been he would have certainly informed the tribunal.

Gulf's approach was mostly a defensive one, confined to repeatedly insisting that the fire had started at 12.55am, but at one point it went very much on the attack in an attempt to undermine evidence given by Garda Patrick Joy. On the fifth day of the hearings, Garda Joy told the tribunal how he had seen the fire on Whiddy at 12.45am while at the West Lodge Hotel. This was not challenged by Gulf lawyers at the time or at any point later, but when Garda Joy returned on the eighteenth day to give evidence about statements he had taken from Gulf employees, he was subjected to a vigorous cross-examination during which it was suggested to him that not only was part of his evidence incorrect but that it was deliberately false. Gulf's allegation was that Garda Joy had told a reporter that he had seen the fire at 12.30am from Bantry Pier, that this was false, and that he had attempted to obtain evidence to support his story by pressurising witnesses to change their opinion about when the disaster started. As the tribunal noted in its report, the allegation "amounted to a charge that the garda attempted to pervert the course of justice . . . and that he deliberately lied in the course of his evidence."

Three newspapers had certainly quoted Garda Joy as saying that he had seen the fire at 12.30am, but on the same day that two of these reports were published the *Evening Press* reported a statement by a senior officer correcting this and establishing that the time given by Garda Joy had in fact been 12.45am. The tribunal in its report said it was satisfied that the garda had never stated that he saw the fire at 12.30am and that while it was impossible to determine how the errors arose in the newspaper reports, it was perfectly understandable that such an error could arise because of the situation that existed in Bantry immediately after the disaster; it was also a mistake that had been speedily corrected and not referred to again.

The tribunal was withering in its dismissal of Gulf's allegations. "The charge made by Gulf was a most serious one. It had no foundation in fact. It was moreover, an inherently improbable one. It should never have been made."

Gulf had also made an attack on how the Gardai had carried out their inquiry into the disaster and in a submission on costs towards the end of the hearings its lawyers claimed that they had "failed in their public duty in the manner in which they had carried out their investigations." The tribunal was having none of it. It considered that the investigation had been carried out "with commendable efficiency and with complete propriety." It concluded: "Again, the tribunal must deprecate the use by Gulf of the tribunal's public hearings to advance baseless and unwarranted criticisms against officials who had manifestly carried out difficult and onerous duties in a thorough and competent manner."

Gulf management had a duty, the tribunal's findings stated, to discover the truth of what happened on the night of the disaster but had failed to fulfil that duty. The management would have been aware from the start that there were eye-witnesses who maintained that the fire had started earlier, and it would have been expected that management would have approached these in their own investigation of the facts. However, they made no such inquiries and did not even take the trouble to contact one of their own employees, James O'Leary, a Whiddy resident who was in a position to give important evidence.

The crucial question must be asked, why were Gulf management not interested, as was clear, in any version of events other than their own? For the tribunal, the answer was simply that the version put forward by Gulf was "highly favourable to their own financial interests." While it did not elaborate on this point, the implication was clear: the 12.55am time for the outbreak of the fire and its rapid spread thereafter meant that little or nothing could have been done to save the lives of the crew or the jetty workers, thus clearing the company of any negligence and reducing the amount of any possible damages.

Gulf management maintained that the 12.55am time was the one given to them at the very start by John Connolly and that they had no reason to doubt it. They also pointed out that his evidence was supported by three other Gulf workers – the skipper of the *Donemark* and two security men – as well as the telephonist in the Bantry telephone exchange. As the tribunal report noted, they "took active steps to ensure that this evidence . . . was not weakened in any way by any official inquiries" and also they had been "highly selective in the sources from which they obtained their information, and were anything but assiduous in seeking out the truth of the events of the disaster."

John Connolly went through an arduous examination at the tribunal over three days, at one point breaking down so that the proceedings had to be discontinued until the following day. Throughout his testimony he insisted that from 10pm on the Sunday night he had not left the control room and at 12.55am had heard "creaking noise" coming from the direction of the jetty. He thought at first it was from the loading arms on the jetty but then saw "the bow of the ship go up in the air" and a small fire appear at the water's edge alongside the ship, which then "got out of all proportions."

To support his evidence, he produced three documents: the first, a sheet of paper on which he had scribbled the time of the fire as it started; the second, two pages from a notebook which he had written between 2.30 and 3am; the third, the control room log, which he had written up at 7am – each of the documents recording the time for the outbreak at 12.55am.

John Connolly's version of events was supported strongly by the skipper of the *Donemark*. According to him, the *Donemark* left Bantry Pier at 12.15am to bring Michael Harris, a cargo inspector with an English company, to the *Betelgeuse* and arrived at Dolphin 22 of the jetty at about 12.40am, after which it proceeded to its moorings at the Ascon jetty. If this was the case, there was obviously no fire at this point on the ship or jetty. The security men on duty that night also insisted in their evidence that the fire could not have started before 12.55am and produced documentary evidence to that effect.

All of this was dismissed out of hand by the report: "The Tribunal concludes that the dispatcher was not in the control room at the commencement of the disaster, and that he decided to suppress this fact and fabricate an account of when and how the disaster occurred. With a view to supporting this version incorrect entries were made in the logs of the control room, the Ascon Jetty security hut and the *Donemark*, and false accounts of the events were given by Gulf employees, both to their employers and to the investigating gardai."

This is the version of events that has established itself as incontrovertible fact, possibly because it was left unchallenged by a media that at the time was more passive and more accepting of the official viewpoint than it is today. It must also be remembered that the media is much more inclined to accept a version of events in which blame is laid on the shoulders of individuals; such a story is much easier to tell and generates more exciting headlines than one that needs to explain complex issues involving corporate or government negligence.

The tribunal's castigation of John Connolly is one that clearly needs to be re-evaluated. It saw him as the instigator of the collusion to suppress the truth, and yet at no time did it consider that this role was in fact played by Gulf Oil management, given the fact that it was the company, as the tribunal itself recognised, that would benefit from the 12.55am time being established as fact, and not any individual. In other words, should it not have considered that the

12.55am time was a concoction by the company and that it had in effect bullied John Connolly and others into going along with this? Such a scenario is certainly not beyond the bounds of possibility, given Gulf's behaviour in other respects.

***

An aspect of the report that was lost among the headlines about the attempts to suppress the truth concerned the role of the various authorities – or, more accurately, their lack of role, since Gulf had from the beginning largely left to its own devices in drawing up rules and procedures about safety and fire-fighting measures without the accepted practice of having these monitored and reviewed by an external body. Right from the beginning, even before construction began on the terminal, there had been demands for the government to set up a harbour authority for Bantry, which would earn fees from Gulf and have a statutory overview of procedures at the terminal. This was strongly resisted, however, and it was clear that the government was anxious to accommodate Gulf as much as possible. The company's assurances that risk of oil spillages and consequent pollution of the bay would be at a minimum, for instance, were taken at face value; moreover, it was argued that since the terminal infrastructure had been developed by Gulf itself, it would simply be wrong to demand fees for the continuing use of the bay, and also that since Gulf would be the only major commercial user of the bay there would be no need for regulating between the conflicting requirements of different users.

This led to a rather bizarre legality, whereby the Department of Transport, in order to conform to a piece of 19th-century legislation dealing with the safe keeping of petroleum, designated Gulf itself as a "harbour authority." Thus the rather strange situation arose in which the company, as the harbour authority, was asked to submit bye-laws relating to the precautions it would take for landing and storing oil and then grant itself a licence for these operations. It all underlined the rather woolly thinking that surrounded the legal aspects of Gulf's presence in Bantry. As it turned out, none of the bye-laws that were first submitted by Gulf in 1968 were accepted, and after a revised draft in 1972 met with a lot of op-

position from other parties with a stake in Bantry Bay, the Minister for Transport decided that operations at Whiddy would be regulated under new legislation then about to be passed by the Dáil, the Dangerous Substances Bill. At first glance, this brought some logic to the situation, allowing the minister to make and enforce the appropriate regulations. In what can only be seen as an exercise in gross political and administrative negligence, however, the regulations were not brought into force until September 1979, seven years after the enabling legislation had been enacted. As a result, according to the tribunal findings, "there was no adequate statutory control of any sort on the movement or storage of petroleum at the terminal or in relation to fire-fighting and safety systems on the jetty." It is impossible not to wonder if, with such regulations in place and properly enforced, the outcome on the night of the disaster would have been very different. The tribunal report had little doubt on this point: "The failure to establish bye-laws . . . or to introduce regulations under the Dangerous Substances Act, 1972, had serious consequences. The statutory obligations placed on Gulf in relation to the maintenance of proper safety measures and standards and the provision of effective fire-fighting systems (particularly in relation to the position of the duty tug) were wholly inadequate. There was a correspondingly inadequate requirement on the public authorities, both at governmental and local level, to supervise and inspect the safety measures and fire-fighting systems at the terminal." The delay in introducing the regulations was, in the view of the tribunal, "extraordinary."

Following a major oil spillage in 1974, the government announced that it would set up a harbour authority for Bantry Bay, and the necessary legislation for this was enacted in 1976. Three years later, at the time of the disaster, it remained a toothless body, being only partly set up and not having any power to deal with the operation of the harbour or to make bye-laws and charge dues.

The report also pointed to a legal anomaly in relation to the role of Cork County Council. As a planning and fire brigade authority, the council's jurisdiction ended at high water mark on Whiddy Island and thus did not extend to the jetty. It was therefore simply not in a position to know of any changes made there that would have a bearing on escape routes or on fire-fighting capabilities. The chief fire officer had raised a comprehensive list of points in 1974 with Gulf, which the company answered in a way that satisfied the council that the facilities were adequate. The company also forwarded a copy of its "Policy and Procedures "manual, from which the fire officer assumed that no change had been made in the mooring position of the duty tug, but this, of course, was not the case..

Over the years I have become more and more convinced that Gulf, whose main objective was to minimise the financial liabilities that followed from the disaster, manipulated John Connolly into a position that made it inevitable that he would become the scapegoat. I have no doubt that there was pressure put on him, as well as on others, to follow the company line on how the night's events unfolded, especially in relation to the time the fire broke out. And it was most likely the same sort of pressure I had been put under: the threat that jobs could be lost if damage was done to the company. I remember clearly how in the weeks and months after the disaster he seemed to be constantly surrounded by members of management no matter where he went, no doubt anxious that he would continue to toe the company line. In fact, I remember him on the morning after the disaster being marched down the corridor by a number of management with the control room log book in hand. It looked like he was getting help to write his log, which turned out to be meticulous and well-polished – unlikely for a man who was under severe pressure.

As a former petty officer in the Navy, he would have been used to taking orders and not questioning those above him. He was a man I respected and found very fair. I don't think he was never the same after the tribunal findings were reported.

I don't believe for a moment that John Connolly was absent from the control room as the tribunal claimed. It was a building I was familiar with and I know that no matter what room you were in off the main control area you would hear everything. My own belief is that John Connolly saw the fire a little after 12.45am and then raised the alarm. But why didn't he see it before that if, as others stated, it had begun even earlier? For a start, as the tribunal report itself said, the fire was initially small and ran along the side of the ship hidden from the view of anyone on the island. This way, it could have been seen by people on the west side of the bay but would not necessarily have been clear to someone in the control room. Also, what was never pointed out, the main control desk at the side of the control panel was to the side of the control room so anyone operating it did not have a clear or immediate view of what was happening on the jetty.

When it came to watching out for emergencies, the controller was not the only person responsible, of course. Others also had this duty, especially those on the jetty or the ship. But was there any alarm raised on the ship or on the jetty when the fire started? Dick Warner and Tim Kingston would have had portable radios with them, and the jetty also had a tannoy system connected directly to the control room. If calls were made over the radio to the control room these would have been heard by the controller, no matter where he was in the building. So is it possible that no immediate alarm was raised because those on the ship and jetty were caught unawares by the rapid spread of the fire? It is also important to understand the nature of an oil fire, that once ignited it gains momentum by the second.

It was the pollution control officer who was in control of all operations; he was there to ensure that everything was being done according to proper procedure. I know also from my own experience as a stand-in jetty foreman that it was our responsibility to feed information back to the control room.

It must be pointed out also that the tribunal's insistence that John Connolly was absent from the control room was not based on any direct evidence whatsoever, but was a conclusion that it arrived at in its own mind, possibly because it helped to tie up all the loose ends. It provided a simple and definite answer to a situation that in reality was much more complex, that wasn't as black and white as the tribunal wished. In the end, all it served to achieve was a grave injustice to a decent man.

The road to recovery

THE WHOLE TRIBUNAL circus came and went, the lawyers shaking the dust of Bantry from their well-shod heels, and I was left to cope with the mess of my own life. It was becoming more difficult by the day. I was supposed to get back to normal life. Everyone else was adjusting, or so it seemed. Why couldn't I?

I continued to work at the terminal, but each journey to the island became increasingly more dif-ficult. Being on Whiddy always brought the mental anguish that was now my constant companion up another notch. I couldn't see anything clearly at the time but, looking back, I find it extraordinary that nobody, neither the people I was working for nor any trade union official, once suggested that I get a medical check immediately after the disaster to see if there were any long-term effects from the prolonged exposure to the all the poison that floated in the air that night. Nor was it suggested that I see a mental health professional, though it must have been certainly clear to them that this was something I badly needed. I could, of course, have sought that help myself, but being mentally unwell brings a confusion that blinds you to this possibility, and it was a confusion that spread to those near me, especially Eleanor, who continued to live on scraps of hope that the man she married would be suddenly and miraculously restored to her. A proper diagnosis at that time would have possibly spared us all the years of torture that were to follow.

What no doubt complicated the whole situation greatly was my increasing dependency on drink. The only thing that could guarantee some sort of a night's sleep was alcohol, but the more I took the more it caused problems in other areas. Eventually when I had the first of my admissions to a psychiatric hospital they gave me medication that helped me to sleep straight away. I think it was valium or something similar. I felt like a new man straight away and wanted to go home immediately, but they kept me another two weeks during which time they diagnosed me as an alcoholic. I told them at length about Whiddy and how I was affected by it afterwards, but they did not seem interested in investigating the possibility of post-traumatic stress, even though they must have been aware of the disorder given the amount of literature on the disorder that was available at the time. Alcoholism, however, was such a convenient, off-the-peg diagnosis of my behaviour that they were reluctant to look beyond it. I don't deny that my relationship with alcohol was a troublesome one and I now know that despite the temporary relief it offered it wasn't doing me any good. But being simply labelled an alcoholic, where everything that was wrong with me was seen as stemming from that condition, just never sat well with me. It was only after Whiddy that I began to drink heavily, and I now see that it was a direct result of my trauma. Alcohol, which after all is a legalised drug, is naturally attractive to anyone under stress, and it is common for people to drink heavily while going through a difficult situation, whether from grief or another type of loss, and then to stop eventually. I think this is the way it was with me, and that the drinking would have gradually subsided with proper treatment for post-traumatic stress. There was one doctor in particular whom I came up against in my admissions to hospital, whose speciality was the treatment of alcoholism. He had undoubtedly huge success in this field, but I felt that because of this he had a vested interest in his chosen subject, and I found that he was the least willing of all to even consider that the roots of my problems could lie elsewhere. We had many stand-up rows. I believe he especially was responsible for delaying my final recovery.

Without proper help, it became inevitable that I would continue to descend into a prolonged emotional hell. I became increasingly withdrawn, constantly burdened by a deep sense of self-loathing. All the other symptoms also continued: insomnia, nightmares, breathing difficulties, blurred vision, leg and back pains, and skin problems.

On my second admission to hospital I was admitted late but, knowing the procedure, I took off my shoes at the front door and tiptoed into the bed that had been made ready for me. I went to sleep fairly quickly thanks to an injection the nurses gave me. The next morning I was confronted by the doctor, the expert on alcoholism, who accused me of being troublesome the previous night and waking up the other patients. Armed with a good night's sleep, I was in better shape to defend myself than in our previous meetings and I challenged him strongly, not something that went down well in a psychiatric ward in those days. His response was to threaten to have me locked up in a mental institution in Cork city. "That'll quieten you," he said. I replied, "Carry on, but I'll be back and I'll quieten you." He said, "Fine, I will have nothing more to do with you" – after which he passed me on to another doctor. That incident with him made me very sceptical about the whole system; what was meant to be a healing process was anything but.

The doctor that I was passed on to, however, was a bit more sympathetic to my case, and not as hung up on the whole alcoholism thing. She was in fact the first to recognise that the root of my problems was in Whiddy and not anywhere else. In a psychiatric report prepared by her she wrote: "In my opinion this patient's symptoms of anxiety and depression can be attributed to the mental trauma he sustained as a result of the January 1979 Whiddy Disaster. Prior to this his mood etc. had always been within normal limits and he had not been on any psychotropic medication."

I HAD TRIED to end my life on two occasions, but it was in the period coming up to my third suicide attempt that I reached a low I had not experienced before. For a while I felt like a completely empty shell and could see no other option but to end everything. Even though I was confused about whether there was a God or not and did not have any great belief in the Catholic Church, I went to a priest and made a lengthy confession but didn't get any ray of hope as I told him everything – except, of course, what I was about to do. I continued to turn it over and over in my mind for about a week to see if there was any way out of it, but the torment got so much that I finally said to myself, "This is the night." I had a big fire on in the range and the water was good and hot. I knew exactly how I was going to do it. The first-aid training I had on Whiddy had taught me where the jugular vein was and I knew that once I cut it with a blade there would be no going back. I would also turn on the shower in the bath to wash away the blood to make it less traumatic for my family. I waited until the whole house was fast asleep before heading to the bathroom. Eleanor, however, unexpectedly woke up and found me with the blade in my hand and managed after a great deal of talking to persuade me to put it away. Somebody, or something, was definitely looking after us that night.

IN JUNE 1981 I quit my job with Gulf Oil despite not having any other job to go to. With the downturn in the level of operations at Whiddy, the company had introduced a voluntary redundancy scheme but I had been against accepting this, as I believed that if we held out we could eventually get a better final payment, and I had made my views known on this to everyone. Turning up for work at the terminal was still emotionally difficult for me even after two years but I was still willing to make a go of it for as long as possible. Things changed suddenly, however, when I was told by a junior member of the management that I had been reported for sleeping while on duty (though at worst I had probably just nodded off for a few seconds) and that I was going to be reprimanded by the company. It was the last straw, and I knew I could not take any more of the pettiness and mean-spirited attitudes that had prevailed at the terminal since the disaster. I told that member of management that I was going to take the voluntary redundancy package, and he told me to write him a note about my decision. I thought that would be the end of it, but then discovered a little later that the company still intended to proceed with disciplinary procedures against me despite the fact that I would soon be leaving their employment. Looking back now with a clearer mind, I can see that they were determined to push me as far as they could in order to get rid of me. It was as clear a case as any of what is known as "constructive dismissal" and something that I could have taken an action over.

In the end, the company failed to pay me the proper voluntary redundancy payment I was due, and it was only after a battle fought on my behalf by a sympathetic official in Social Services that I managed to get what I was legally entitled to in the first place.

There were times when I thought that I would have a better chance of getting back to my old self once I got away from Whiddy. But that was naive thinking, and instead I fell into another mental tailspin, made worse by having no regular wage packet and with the bills mounting up. After about two years of this misery and a number of hospital admissions, some people, including a doctor who had been treating me, suggested to me that I take advice from a local solicitor to see if Gulf would be willing to grant me some sort of compensation, particularly in light of the role I had played on the night of the disaster – a role that had been commended in the media and in the tribunal report itself. Surely, I was told by so many, the company would be prepared to help someone who had been harmed while working for them. Gulf, however, strenuously resisted the claim, arguing through their lawyers that although the "underlying facts of my case were not without merit", my claim had been filed statutorily too late. At this point I also began to receive messages indirectly from management that if I proceeded with taking a case "things would get much worse for me".

In short, rather than do the honourable thing by me, the company had seized onto a legal technicality to avoid responsibility, saying that I should have pressed my claim within two years of the disaster. If the case went to trial that technicality would automatically ensure that my claim would be dismissed. It would be possible in that event, of course, to mount a challenge under the Constitution to any such judgement, but going that route would be costly and beyond my resources, so I reluctantly abandoned the claim.

I thought that would be the end of the matter, but, to add to my humiliation, Gulf then demanded that I pay the legal costs. It seemed they were legally entitled to do this because the case had just one mention in court. I didn't have the will or the strength at this stage to fight them on this (which I now realise I should have done) and I pleaded with them to drop the costs, which they did, but only after I signed a document promising not to bring any legal action against them in the future.

IN 1986 THE government announced a special development package worth millions for West Cork, with a special emphasis on Bantry. This was definitely a welcome and much-needed boost for the area, yet I couldn't help feel that yet again the full extent of the damage caused by the disaster was not being addressed. For four years the state had devoted extensive resources to salvage the devastated physical environment of Whiddy. Why should any less effort have been expended in order to salvage the individual human wreckage?

The nub of the problem, I believe, lay in the tribunal's narrow definition of the term "loss of life". Certainly that does mean death, but it should also take into consideration other ways in which someone can be robbed of his or her life. Life is about living, but it is also about living with dignity, which no one has the right to take away from you.

THE FIRST PERSON who really made a break-through with me was Sister Eileen O'Sullivan who in the late 1980s had been given permission by her order to return to her home in Castledonovan to look after her ailing father. She had a reputation as a saintly woman and as a healer. Someone I had become friends with in hospital knew all about her and felt she could do something for me. I wasn't having any of it. I had never stopped practising my religion, but I had always done it in a superficial, conventional sort of way, and I had little time for anything that smacked of spirituality, certainly not anything like spiritual healing. In the end, my friend managed to get me to visit her by asking if I would do a job in her house, something to do with the electrics. As soon as I met her I knew she was different, that she had a compassion and an understanding that I had never experienced in anyone else; I sensed immediately that this was someone who really listened. We began to talk, and I opened up as best I could to tell her about everything that had happened to me. She then asked me to forgive the people who had caused me so much pain and anguish. "I can't," I said. "I am not a hypocrite." She answered me in a way I didn't expect. "I really love you for your honesty," she said.

The following week I returned to the house after receiving an invitation from her to attend a healing session, this time bringing along my mother-in-law who was then quite ill. I felt Sister Eileen perhaps could do something for her, but I didn't expect anything would work for me as I was convinced I was a lost cause. While the healing sessions were continuing I began to wander around the house aimlessly and at one point when I was passing her door she invited me in. We talked for a while and then she laid her hands on me and prayed. The effect was immediate. A tremendous heat ran through my body, and I felt as if I was in a boat being gently rocked back and forth; a profound, unfamiliar peace fell over me.

A long period of relative tranquillity followed, perhaps a few years, but without realising it there were other problems I was going to have to tackle – problems that arose from my childhood and had lain hidden for so long. The changes for the worse were subtle and gradual until I found myself back in the hell I thought I had left forever. I began to become physically ill, I was losing weight, I was developing allergies, and I found it increasingly difficult to hold onto the gift of spirituality I got from God through Sister Eileen. All the old symptoms of post-traumatic stress resurfaced, and it was recommended that I go on what was then being hailed a new wonder drug, Prozac. But it didn't work, and I felt abandoned again in a black hole of despair.

Even though I had lost all sense of hope and wanted only to die, Eleanor refused to give up on me. In 1991 she heard about a psychologist and counsellor called Michael Hardiman who had a great success rate helping people with severe depression. I resisted her suggestions to go and see him, being tired at this stage of spinning wheels with psychiatrists and psychologists. In the end, however, I reluctantly agreed to talk to him.

At my first meeting with Michael I told him that if I wasn't able to do something about the continual mental torture and lack of sleep I would be dead within two years. "You're wrong," he said. "It will take much less time than that."

I continued in therapy with Michael for about a year and again, as had happened at least temporarily with Sister Eileen, I began the journey out of my personal hell. My faith, which to this day continues to be at the very centre of my life, began to deepen again, and I learned that God would not do for me what I was meant to do myself. I now knew that I would have to do the repairing, but He would give me the grace and strength to go though the pain.

The grace and strength was certainly needed to deal with something else I learned through my sessions with Michael – that what had happened on Whiddy that awful night had, as it were, fractured the very foundation of my life and opened up a crack through which the untreated trauma of my childhood had surfaced to swamp all my thoughts and feelings and prevent any real chance of long-term recovery. With his help and encouragement, however, I began to put a new foundation in place and build my life back together brick by brick. It was not an easy task and it brought me down some unexpected routes, including investigating my family history where I was to discover much pain and loss. The Biblical phrase,

"The sins of the fathers . . ." sprung to mind on a number of occasions. This part of my life brought a series of strange experiences, including vivid images of faces appearing to me, which were unfamiliar but which I felt had some strong connection with. After this happened a few times I began to sense that what they were seeking was for me to forgive them. Once I did this, they disappeared, never to return.

ON 15 AUGUST 2007 I received out of the blue a letter from Dr Mary T. O'Mahony, a specialist in public health medicine in the Department of Public Health, HSE-South. The letter bowled me over for two reasons: firstly, the insight it had into my condition was extraordinary; secondly, I was totally perplexed about how this doctor knew so much about me in the first place.

As it turned out, a copy of a letter I had sent in September 2006 to President Mary McAleese and to Bertie Ahern as Taoiseach, had been passed onto Dr O'Mahony. In this letter I explained what had happened to me and how I had been left down by the state, and I also raised concerns about the lack of action over possible public health hazards in the immediate aftermath of the disaster, which is why Dr O'Mahony was asked to comment on it. Her letter included a report of an analysis she had done on my letter.

The analysis began, "Mr McGee's letter is an extremely well articulated and poignantly elucidated account of his experience of the Gulf Oil Whiddy Island Disaster and its immediate and consequent effect on his life. However, it is written as a statement of a series of facts, as though from a remove, seeking understanding rather than sympathy. I read his letter several times and have tried to answer these questions: How does he feel he has suffered? How does he feel he has been left down? What is he looking for?"

Her conclusions were as follows:

"Mr McGee suffered physically and psychologically in the immediate aftermath of the disaster. He also suffered in the long term, particularly psychologically. It should be noted however that his psychological suffering has left a very physical imprint, his psychological distress has left him unable to sleep, 'destroyed from drink', and suicidal.

"Perhaps the single cause of all his suffering and feelings of being let down stem from being left alone. He was left to his own devices from the very beginning, he had no protective gear while fighting the fire, and much of the fire fighting equipment was 'useless'. His sense of isolation and abandonment only increased with time as societal and Church supports declined as 'normalcy' resumed. Life as he knew it had changed completely; his 'own self was dead'. Every structure that he believed in – society, church, the state – had failed him, with the ultimate hurt being that the Irish Constitution, which he had hoped would be there for him, was actually the instrument used to beat him.

"He is disappointed and disillusioned, but arguably, not completely without hope. He has addressed his letter to the two highest authorities of the state. It is my reading of his letter that Mr McGee hoped the inquiry would somehow find an explanation or reason for all that had happened to him, and perhaps give him a reason for having lived or even thank him for helping. He has questioned why he has survived.

"Mr McGee has outlined how it affected him, and

seeks recognition that he sacrificed so much of his life for Gulf Oil, Total Oil SA, Cork County Council, and Ireland. He wants to be acknowledged as a person, a citizen, a life. He needs the faith he put in society, the state, and the mechanisations of the State reciprocated.

"His tragedy has not been recognised, and it is this that haunts him. At the time he needed someone to ask him how it affected him. He might still need someone to ask him but certainly to hear him. Most simply, although he has said how it affected him, he needs to be asked."

Dr O'Mahony, in the letter that accompanied this analysis, also said, "It is clear that . . . you showed commitment to duty and demonstrated personal courage in staying at the fire-fighting task while feeling great fear. I note that you continue to suffer from post-traumatic stress disorder and survivor's guilt . . . I wish you well in your personal journey."

As for my letter to the President and the Taoiseach, I was extremely disappointed at the manner in which it was treated. I had the impression that neither of them had bothered to read it but had passed it on to numerous departments until it ended up with the HSE, who received it on 10 January 2007, nearly four months later. The HSE's response was in August 2007, eleven months to the day from the date of my original letter. I did ask the HSE why there was such a long delay in responding, and they advised that the final report and analysis was signed off on 18 April 2007, but additional time was taken to reflect on the analysis and do the public health risk assessment. I would stress that my comments above are not a criticism of the HSE, as I was very grateful to Dr O'Mahony for the interest and commitment she gave to my situation.

I did receive an acknowledgement from the President's secretariat dated 19 September in which she referred to the Whiddy Island Disaster of 8 January 2006. This careless mistake about the date of the disaster told me that my letter had not been treated in any serious manner, but merely put in the out tray along with a covering letter. The letter stated the following, "However, I would like to explain that the President is constrained by the constitutional requirements of her office, and cannot intervene in areas which come within the remit of the Government."

There was a time when Mary McAleese was a current affairs reporter for RTE's *Frontline* programme and was fiercely dedicated to covering the horror that was the Whiddy Island disaster. Bureaucratic and corporate dissembling did not deter her, nor was she uninterested in individual victims and community tragedies. With that background, I thought the least she could have done was to give me some moral support. How times change!

IT WASN'T UNTIL after thirty years – in January 2009 – that a memorial service was finally held to remember the dead and to bring together the bereaved and the survivors from that tragic night. The truth is that it might never have been held unless I had got a few others to join me in a campaign for such a commemoration.

A GREAT ALLY in my campaign was Ann O'Leary, a Sinn Féin councillor, who persuaded the more reluctant members of Bantry Town Council to do something and prevent the calamity from slipping into total obscurity, which would have been an insult to the memory of those who died and their families.

As far back as 1994 I had sent a letter, co-signed by eight others, to the then mayor of Bantry, Pat Bonna Kelly, to urge the Town Council to institute a yearly Whiddy memorial service, just as had been done for the victims of the Air India crash in 1985. We never received a reply

In 2004, the twenty-fifth anniversary of the disaster, the town council debated at length the possibility of having a memorial service that year, but despite all the talk nothing came of it. The following year, I renewed my efforts and wrote to the new mayor, Letty Baker, urging her and the council to look again at the possibility of holding a service to remember the "many dead and to honour those dedicated persons whose efforts prevented a much wider catastrophe." I also reminded her of her contribution to the council debate on the matter when she had suggested that the council should host a photographic and educational exhibition "lest the citizenry gradually forget the historical significance and personal sacrifice of that terrible night."

Not long after sending this letter I was given to

understand that she had issued a directive to the town clerk that I be directly involved in some fashion with the organization of a memorial service. However, I was never once approached to participate nor notified of any schedule or timetable of memorial events once the council had got the ball rolling. In fact, I didn't even receive an invitation. It was all deeply hurtful and it caused me immense stress. Was it that they felt uncomfortable with having someone around who was prepared to ask awkward questions?

At some point later, Alex Donovan, the Bantry harbour master, approached me in a coffee shop and informed me that the town council and harbour authority had formed a committee to organise and promote the thirtieth anniversary of the disaster. I was under the impression that I would be kept informed of progress but I never was, and this was the last I heard anything about it until close to the day itself in 2009.

Despite the snub, I went to the memorial service at the *Betelgeuse* monument, hidden away in the Abbey graveyard. Each time I see it, I am reminded of the statue in the Square of St Brendan which Gulf put up in the late 1960s, and how some people cheered about the good times to come to Bantry and the money they would make. I then attended the Mass for the bereaved during which a message from Mary McAleese was read out. Her words of sympathy came across to me as hypocrisy, and I felt like walking out of the church, but was seated too far up the aisle to make an exit. The hardest part was that none of us who had risked our lives on Whiddy that night were mentioned at any point. It was if we did not exist.

Before the service started I got talking to two reporters outside the church. When they heard I had been on Whiddy on the night of the disaster, they arranged to meet me later at the reception in the West Lodge Hotel. But when I got there, they ignored me completely. It was as if someone had got to them and warned them that I was some sort of crank.

It was just another blow in a long line of such over the years. Such things still hurt deeply, but at least I have come to realse that trying to tell the truth doesn't go down well with certain types of people. And thus it will always be.

Trying to get at the truth about Whiddy and about

myself is what this book is about. For a long time I have felt between a rock and a hard place about it. Although I knew that I had no option but to write it, I also knew it would put me through hell again.

I may have learned to forgive, but I can never forget, and each memory brings its own pain. I thank the Lord and his blessed Mother for all the grace and strength that has been given to me over the years, because from that fateful night on I had very little to lean that I could call my own.

I never saw the footprints but I know in my heart that the good Lord was carrying me. I now realise that life is a gift from God, not one minute of which should be wasted.

I know I cannot be what I was but I can hold on to what is left and hope that it sees me through the rest of my life. Sometimes, however, it is like trying to hold on to smoke. But the one thing I know, and which I sensed before that night in January 1979, is that life is, indeed, full of possibilities.

APPENDIX
'Why I quit the Inquiry'

DR H.K. BLACK *spent the whole of his career as a consulting scientist in the area of dangerous substances. He was chief inspector of explosives in the UK Home Office for eleven years and acted as adviser to the Home Secretary and licensing authorities on petroleum safety measures. He was responsible for inquiries into many accidents, including the great fire at W. London Petroleum Terminal in 1968. The following is the statement he issued after resigning as a special adviser to the Whiddy Tribunal:*

I withdrew for two reasons: first, that I had never before heard such evidence as was given by some witnesses and, secondly, restrictions were imposed on me in questioning others. I was unable, therefore, to carry out the task for which I was appointed. This has resulted in some witnesses being released without the most important questions being put to them and, in consequence, answers to these questions are now lost to the Tribunal. No doubt this will occur again and so for my own reputation I had no option but to withdraw.

Now some points out of many that could be dealt with. The design of the Terminal was fundamentally wrong, for no sufficient safeguards existed in operations, in fire-fighting and in evacuation of personnel. The fire equipment and fire-fighting arrangements, ashore and on the platform, were such as to rend it imperative to close down until the defects were remedied. The emergency evacuation of personnel had not been seriously considered, nor had recent training taken place. This was an island jetty with no land escape route, but only access by sea, and as such it demanded, and did not get, the most rigid safeguards for the protection of personnel.

The arrangements for dealing with fires on the

jetty were ludicrous; the fire mains could only be energised from the control room (or ashore). For reasons not yet explained, there seems to have been a delay between the time when the fire might be presumed to have started and Control becoming aware of it. In this situation the platform crew had no means of fighting the fire, nor were there any means in the then circumstances whereby they could be rescued. And they could not help themselves because I doubt very much whether anyone knew how to use the life-raft on Dolphin 22, or had even seen it demonstrated. Apart from that, the Company was living in a fool's paradise if it thought that a life-raft would be of any significant help other than in ideal weather conditions, and probably in daytime.

In regard to the Dispatcher, he worked a twelve-hour shift, and alone. He was the key man, the linchpin, on whom everything depended in the event of an accident. I do not believe that any man can remain fully alert during such a period, particularly at night. No man should be expected to work such long hours and to shoulder alone the enormous responsibility that the Dispatcher has to bear. It is a very grave reflection on the Company that they expected him to do so.

It would seem that they had even got the hazardous areas classification wrong. If the platform had really been Division 0, the toxic nature of the petroleum vapours would have prevented work on it. Moreover, who would ever contemplate operations in a Division 0 area?

On the platform was a pressurised room. No one in his right mind would put such a room in a Division 0 area. Even in a Division 1 area, which should have been the real classification of the platform, where it would be allowable, the actual room was dangerous – and no one seems to have been aware of it.

The ship was berthed into the wind, which is contra-indicated in an accommodation-aft vessel. Any vapours or fire would be blown towards the accommodation where most of the crew were asleep. The stern was soon engulfed in flame, but the bow section remained untouched. Had the ship been berthed the other way round, I think it is quite likely that most of the crews would have been saved for Dolphin was unaffected by fire, as was part of the jetty towards it.

I am not a ship expert, but I expect the experts to find that the condition of the ship, and the ballasting programme, were such as to make the breaking of its back a predictable event, certainly if the evidence were to show that it was preceded by a minor explosion in the 4a wing tanks.

There is no need for me to go into the serious deficiencies of the Manuals, or to comment on the devastating electrical and mechanical reports on the jetty, nor need I refer to the management or to the lack of local or central government control , for I have already said enough to indicate that there was a very great deal wrong on the ship and ashore. I can only speculate on the reasons that prevented me from making a full inquiry into the aspects that were of the greatest importance. I only know one way of inquiring into serious accidents, and that is to pursue the truth as fairly and honestly as I can without fear and without favour to anyone. I can only regret that I was not permitted to do so.

Meantime, I am astonished at the course of the Inquiry, in the light of the Resolution and the debate thereon in which grave concern was expressed as to reasons which led to the death of 51 persons in the most horrendous circumstances that can be imagined. It was an accident that should never have been allowed to happen but, having occurred, there should have existed, and there could have existed, plans and arrangements whereby some, if not all the personnel, could have been saved.

An enormous amount of work will have to be done if ever the Terminal is reconstituted, in order to put it onto a satisfactory basis. Harbour bye-laws will need to be promulgated, a Code of Practice set up, and entirely revised Operations and disaster Manuals prepared. Personnel fully trained in petroleum technology will be required. It will be essential to exercise central government control and inspection.

On 6 October I notified Mr Justice Costello of my withdrawal and my reasons for it. On 16 October he replied that he had received my letter and noted its contents. I would hope to find, and indeed I would expect to find, a different standard of behaviour amongst his colleagues on the Bench.

In memoriam

French victims

Roger Hamono, Master

René Bazin, Master

François Mourrain, Chief Mate

Michel Gibert, Mate

Loíc Allegre, Mate

Marcel Ravaleu, Mate

Louis Lelievre, Radio Officer

Paul Moyon, Chief Engineer

Gaston Dorso, 2nd Engineer

Claude Quintard, 3rd Engineer

Christian Melenec, 4th Engineer

Yves Le Baccon, 5th Engineer

Pierre Camus, Boatswain

Michel Prod'homme, Carpenter

Paul Salaun, Pumpman

Jean Brelivet, Petty Officer

Jean François Parravicini, Petty Officer

Robert Le Page, Able Seaman

Bernard Danielou, Able Seaman

Nicolas Bolore, Able Seaman

Yvon Le Perff, Able Seaman

Christian Leonard, Able Seaman

Honorin Jermidi, Able Seaman

Pierre Le Coquen, Chief Steward

Marc Hericher, Chief Cook

Louis Lassale, Baker

Denis Dufoulon, Galley Boy

Charles Cassand, Steward

Pierre Huet, Steward

Eugène Moriniaux, Electrician

René Tanter, Assistant Engineer

Maurice Le Guennec, Greaser

Henri Rogel, Greaser

Yves Thual, Greaser

Gabriel Heurtel, Greaser
Pierre Robin, Greaser
Ibrahima Traore, Cleaner
Jacky Davy, Cadet
Jean Spitzbarth, Electro Officer
Marcelle Lassale, Baker's Wife
Dominique Pochic, Steward
Emmanuel Camenen, Technical Superintendent

Irish victims
Timothy Kingston, Pollution Control Officer
David Warner, Ship's Pilot
James O'Sullivan, Jetty Foreman
Denis O'Leary, Plant Protection Operator
Charles Brennan, Jetty Utilityman
William Shanahan, Jetty Utilityman
Cornelius O'Shea, Jetty Utilityman

English victim
Michael Harris, Cargo Inspector

www.ingramcontent.com/pod-product-compliance
Lightning Source LLC
Chambersburg PA
CBHW051839090426
42736CB00011B/1883